THE LORD'S TAVERNERS

Message from The President of The Lord's Taverners

I am delighted to be asked to write a brief welcome to "The Lord's Taverners Little Book of Cricket". I guarantee you will find it a good read with something for everyone.

Those not familiar with The Lord's Taverners may like to know that we started life as a club, founded in 1950 by a group of actors who used to enjoy a pint watching the cricket from the Old Tavern pub at Lord's.

Today, we are now both a club and a charity and recognised as cricket's official charity. As well as The Lord's Taverners we have two other separate fundraising arms - The Lady Taverners (founded 1987) and The Young Lord's Taverners (founded 1988). The charity also incorporates the Brian Johnston Memorial Trust, which supports blind cricket in particular.

Since 1950 we have given away more than £35 million in grant aid, of which 50% goes to support youth cricket in the UK, 35% to supplying recreational transport (minibuses) for organisations supporting disabled young people and 15% to supplying sports and recreational equipment for young people with special needs, which includes wonderful projects like Table Cricket.

The Taverners like having fun whilst fundraising aiming to give away all the money we raise each year. In 2004 our grants amounted to more than £2 million. By buying this little book you are helping us make a big difference to a lot of young people!

Mike Gatting OBE
www.lordstaverners.org

THE LITTLE BOOK OF
CRICKET

This edition first published in the UK in 2005
By Green Umbrella
www.greenumbrella.co.uk

© Green Umbrella Publishing 2004

Publishers Jules Gammond, Tim Exell

Printed and bound in Hong Kong

ISBN 1 905009 00 3

Contents

Ashes

THE ASHES ARE THE OLDEST and – despite Australia's world dominance in recent years – most venerated contest in cricket. The match now accepted as the first Test ever played was in Melbourne in 1877. Australia beat England by 45 runs, a margin coincidentally repeated when the two sides met on the same ground 100 years later. But the idea of the Ashes was not born until 1882, when England lost a low-scoring classic at The Oval amid such tension that one spectator allegedly chewed through the handle of his umbrella.

Who knows whether the famous urn would have eventually come into being had not Dr WG Grace, England's Champion, been called to a case when he should have been padding up, pre-cipitating a ten-minute delay. According to contemporary lore, George Eber Spendlove died of a haemorrhage despite Grace's ministrations, no doubt upsetting the Doctor's equilibrium. Although he top-scored with 32 in England's second innings, "The Demon" Frederick Spofforth took the honours for Australia with 14 wickets in the match.

A few days later the following obituary notice appeared in "The Sporting Times":

In Affectionate Remembrance
OF
ENGLISH CRICKET,
WHICH DIED AT THE OVAL
ON
29th AUGUST, 1882,
Deeply lamented by a large circle of sorrowing
friends and acquaintances.

R. I. P.

N.B.—*The body will be cremated and the
ashes taken to Australia.*

So they became a subliminal notion, and reality soon followed. Amid general recrimination following England's defeat, the Honourable Ivo Bligh offered to take a team to Australia for three matches the following winter. At a dinner in Melbourne, which preceded the series, Bligh rose to reveal the nature of his quest. "We have come to beard the kangaroo in his den, and try to recover those Ashes."

Although the reference met with general mystification, Bligh was as good as his word. England came back from a nine-wicket defeat in the opener to win the series two-one, but it was a legendary encounter at Rupertswood - the country home in Sunbury of millionaire rancher Sir William Clarke - which proved to have far-reaching consequences both for Anglo-Australian rivalry and for Bligh himself. He was introduced to Miss Florence Rose Morphy, a music teacher to Sir William's family, who was sufficiently interested in the game to follow the fortunes of Bligh and England in the ensuing series.

What perplexed her and other ladies of the household was how England could be in Australia playing for a trophy that did not actually exist. So after the third Test they burnt a bail, or perhaps a ball, or possibly Florence's veil, as stated by her 82-year-old daughter-in-law in 1998. They placed the ashes in a tiny urn,

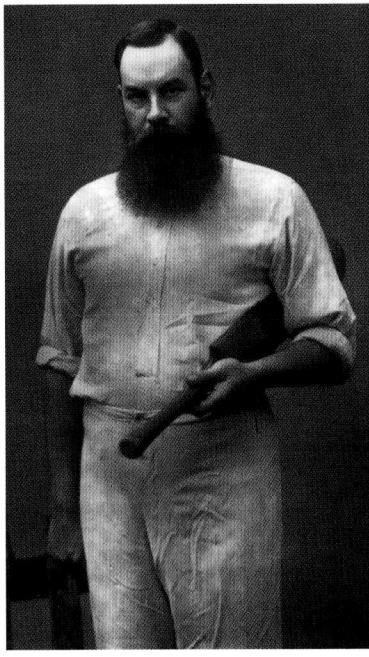

BELOW The most famous of them all, W.G. Grace

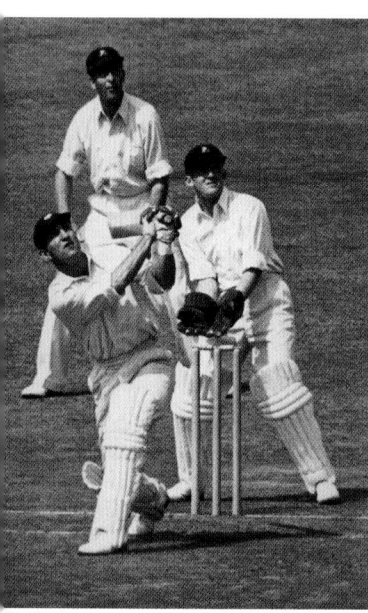

ABOVE Len Hutton hits out on his way to his momentous 364

which they duly presented to Bligh. As a romantic footnote, he later married Florence and the two lived as the Earl and Countess of Darnley at Cobham Hall in England, where Bligh took the urn.

Two years after his death in 1927, the Countess bequeathed it to the MCC. But the fame of its contents might be said to have flickered only gradually into life, while the unending struggle for supremacy between England and Australia was already assuming Herculean proportions. England were to retain the Ashes over another seven series and almost a decade after 1882/3, but since then Australia have had much the better of successive contests. They held them for a record 19 years (admittedly including the Second World War) from 1934, another 12 from 1953, and after regular exchanges in the 1970s and 80s, they have retained them since 1989.

Records abound, both collective and individual. There was England's monumental 903 for seven at The Oval in 1938, built around Len Hutton's 364, which eclipsed even Don Bradman's 334 made at Headingley eight years earlier. Bradman's genius is reflected in the fact that he still features in the most prolific Ashes partnerships (with Ponsford, Fingleton, Hassett and Barnes) for the second, third, fourth, fifth and sixth wickets. And England's incomparable Walter Hammond looms large between the wars (251 and 231 not out at Sydney, and 240 at Lord's). More recently, both David Gower and Nasser Hussain have passed the 200 mark.

Of the bowlers, Jim Laker's stupendous feat in taking 19 Australian wickets at Manchester in 1956 remains unsurpassed, as does his tally of 46 wickets in the five-Test series. Even over six Tests Terry Alderman, such a thorn in England's side in the 1980s, could not better that (he took 42 wickets in the legendary 1981 rubber, when Ian Botham's return to form carried England to victory). And Mike Gatting won't need reminding about the "ball of the century" from Shane Warne, the leg-spinner's first in Ashes cricket, which turned almost square to hit the stumps.

OPPOSITE Jim Laker sends down another ball during the 1956 Ashes series

BELOW Ian Botham swings at a ball from Geoff Lawson of Australia on his way to his sensational 149*during the third Test match at Headingley, 1981

The passion generated by the contest has at times exceeded what many would term reasonable limits, most infamously in the Bodyline series of 1932/3, when Douglas Jardine's adoption of "leg theory" fast bowling injured diplomatic relations as well as Australian batsmen. A more recent encounter degenerated into near farce when Dennis Lillee, already established as one of the game's greatest fast bowlers, elected to showcase an aluminium bat in a Test match at Perth. The England captain, Mike Brearley, was not amused, and the bat's useful life proved strictly limited.

The remarkable history of the urn itself has not been without incident in the past decade. Amid gathering calls for whoever holds the Ashes to hold the urn as well, MCC commissioned a Waterford glass trophy of greater size but identical shape, which was first presented to the Australian captain Mark Taylor after the 1998-99 series. It has been presented to the winning captain at the end of each series since. The original urn has undergone extensive restoration after damage was caused to the stem by adhesive from a previous repair, and although there are plans for it to be displayed in Australia, it is now reinstated in the MCC Museum at Lord's, its home for over 75 years.

BELOW The new Waterford glass trophy with the original urn

Bat & Ball

TO SEARCH FOR THE ORIGINS OF these two indispensable implements, it is necessary to make a cursory foray back towards the birth of the game itself. Not that it is possible to arrive at a specific point, since the exact origins will surely be shrouded in mystery forever. For all the talk of Hambledon and Broadhalfpenny Down as where it all started, there is evidence of the game's existence before the end of the 16th century.

It is quite conceivable that it began as a contest between stick and a piece of wood, both then widely available in the downlands of southeast England. Nor is it hard to imagine a contest between shepherds in those early days, with the bat a shepherd's crook and ball of wound cloth – presumably wool. To carry this imaginary scenario a fraction further, what better wicket could

there have been than the wicket gate of a sheep pen?

Whatever the exact origins, how did the bat and ball evolve into what we have now? In both cases the process was a gradual one. The chunk of wood became one of more spherical shape, and later still a piece of cork, or some other form of stuffing, with a leather covering stitched around it. That was the prototype for today's ball, which is made of hand-stitched leather dyed red or white, with an interior of cork wound with twine. Regulations concerning size and weight followed, which have changed marginally over the years.

ABOVE A 1768 portrait of a boy holding a cricket bat by Francis Cotes

Back in 1744, the only thing that mattered about the ball was its weight, which could be no less than five ounces and no more than six. Thirty years later this was

narrowed down to between five and a half ounces (155.9 grams) and five and three-quarter ounces (163g). A ruling on the ball's circumference followed in 1838, specified as between nine and nine and a quarter inches. In 1927 this was reduced to the present-day figure, no less than eight and thirteen-sixteenths of an inch (22.4 centimetres), and no greater than nine inches (22.9 cm). The balls used in women's cricket are slightly smaller and lighter, and for Under-13 cricket still more so (four and three-quarter ounces).

Within these parameters there are regional variations. Balls can behave differently depending on their make, and on the prevailing conditions. The Kookaburra ball, for example, rapidly ceases to assist the bowler after around 20 overs of a match. The captain can take a new ball after a minimum of 75 overs; in most current international cricket it is after 80. Balls may go out of shape from time to time, although the views of the bowler and umpire on this can contrast widely. The bowler may simply be hoping to get a ball replaced because it isn't "doing" as much as he thinks it should. It is often a delicate judgement for the umpire, who is the final arbiter in such matters.

So much for the ball - how did the bat develop from a mere stick off a tree, or shepherd's crook, into the comparatively sophisticated wand that is wielded at present? It was honed into a club, which itself evolved into something akin to a hockey stick, designed to deal with the under-arm deliveries of earlier days, propelled all along the ground in a literal derivation of the original "bowling". The first signs of a shoulder emerged with the "batten bat", and the now customary splice followed.

Today, the bat's blade is made of willow, while the handle comprises strips of cane layered with rubber, the whole bound with twine and encased in one or more rubber grips. The splice is the extension of the cane from the shoulder of the willow into the meat of it. The back of the bat contrasts with the front; typically it is rounded, although in modern bats a scoop might be taken out of the middle, or various other incursions made at the back to distribute the weight for better balance and a larger 'middle'.

For obvious reasons, the bat's dimensions are limited. It can be no more than four and a quarter inches (10.8 cm) in width, and 38 inches (96.5 cm) in height. Following Dennis Lillee's notorious

ABOVE Cricket equipment suppliers Duncan Fearnley still practice the noble art of bat-making

ABOVE LEFT Dennis Lillee is questioned by England captain Mike Brearley about his unusual and ultimately illegal aluminium bat

experiment with an aluminium bat at Perth in 1980, the MCC inserted a clause into the Laws of Cricket stipulating that the blade must be made of wood. However there is no restriction on weight, nor has there ever been. While four-pound bats were once commonplace, the weight nowadays tends to range from two and a half to three pounds. Protective covering, as a means of strengthening or repair, is also permitted, provided it 'shall not be likely to cause unacceptable damage to the ball'.

Another law of critical relevance to the bat concerns the hand and glove of the batsman, both of which are deemed to be part of the bat itself. Many a marginal dismissal has resulted, with batsmen escaping because a brush on the glove was invisible and inaudible to the umpire, or being wrongly given out caught off the armguard or some other piece of protective kit. In 2001 the talented Pakistan batsman Yousuf Youhana was most unfortunate to be given out caught at slip off the peak of his helmet, rather than his bat or glove. It was just one more dismissal of somewhat freakish quality, in which the bat was adjudged to have been involved but in fact was not.

Naturally the bat manufacturers want their own names to be clearly visible, particularly in the age of zoom lenses and close-up photography. Established names such as Slazenger, Gunn and Moore, Duncan Fearnley and Gray Nicolls appear in their distinctive logos, as does the more recently established Woodworm brand, endorsed by the magnificent England all-rounder Andrew Flintoff. In India, tobacco companies have been known to circumvent advertising regulations by using the logo of a brand of cigarettes on bats used by leading players while, at the same time, producing a very limited number of similar bats for general sale.

For established international players, the benefits of endorsement are huge, with bats as with other visible equipment, although one of the more memorable cricket pictures of recent years is of the then Australian captain Steve Waugh, hobbling with a calf injury against England at The Oval in 2001, diving to achieve the run which completed his century. Raised aloft, like a periscope from the sea, was his bat in acknowledgement of the applause, and not a sponsor or a maker's name in sight. What a throwback to the good old days!

ABOVE Steve Waugh celebrates his 2001 Oval century with a strangely bare bat

OPPOSITE Andrew Flintoff salutes a one-day hundred against Sri Lanka in 2004, his Woodworm bat raised to the crowd

Captaincy

THE JOB OF A CAPTAIN in most sports is not terribly demanding. In football, for example, he might have to toss the coin and be available to speak to the media after the match, and he will probably act as a conduit between players and management. The good ones will be able to inspire the players around them, but they are unlikely to be responsible for tactical changes in play.

The rugby captain has rather more influence on the field when it comes to strategic thinking, and can certainly bring motivational powers to bear along with everything else. The captain of a golf team, as in the Ryder Cup, does not actually take part in the playing of the match, but is more of a coach or manager than is usually recognised by the word captain.

When it comes to cricket, however, the captain's role is different. Apart from tossing the coin, talking to the media, acting as that conduit referred to earlier and playing a vital role in strategy, he also has a few other jobs to do. He has to be diplomat, psychologist, motivator, man-manager, mathematician, tactician, weather forecaster, selector, lawyer, gambler, philosopher and, in many cases, nursemaid. Add to that the underlying requirement that he should be a player worthy of a place in the team and it becomes evident that captaincy in cricket is one of the most demanding tasks in sport.

Cricket is a complex game and requires astute tactical thinking. An analogy could be drawn to a general manoeuvring his army in battle. If that appears to be overstating the case, examine the contents of a losing captain's postbag. You will see that the consequences of losing a cricket match and a battle are regarded by many as being of parallel importance. On the sub-continent, a losing captain who is thought to be responsible for defeat can expect his house to be attacked and his effigy to be burnt in the streets. All the while, the winning captain might have to move to a bigger house just to accommodate all the rewards that come with success.

Despite the inescapable fact that a captain will be praised or damned for the performance of his team, there are limits to the control he can exert. Although he might have done everything he could and met all the criteria bar one, there has yet to be a great cap-

tain of a losing team. The one criterion he has failed to meet is that of winning. Similarly, a captain with a world-beating team at his disposal can be excused for concealing the fact that his maiden aunt could do the job just as well.

It might be considered unfortunate for some very able leaders that their captaincy skills do not attract the accolades that might be warranted because of the strength of the teams they command. Clive Lloyd was undoubtedly such a case. Although a fine captain, his skills as a leader were seldom tested for the mere fact that he had such a powerful array of talent available to play for him.

OPPOSITE Graeme Smith of South Africa wins the toss whilst Michael Vaughan and Clive Lloyd look on in the opening Test of their 2004/5 series

BELOW England captain Nasser Hussain manoeuvres his troops during the 2002 Lord's Test match against Sri Lanka

ABOVE West Indies' legendary captain Clive Lloyd in action against India in 1983

It could be argued that a team sheet that reads: Greenidge, Haynes, Richardson, Gomes, Richards, Lloyd himself and the wicket-keeper Dujon to bat and Marshall, Holding, Garner and Walsh to bowl does not really need a captain. The same could be said of Steve Waugh's Australians. It is a captain's dream to see the asterisk by his name in a line-up that includes Hayden, Langer, Ponting, Mark Waugh, Steve Waugh, Martyn, Gilchrist, Warne, Lee, Gillespie and McGrath. A match between those two sides at the peak of their powers is one to be played on the Elysian Fields. It would certainly test the two leaders' powers of captaincy.

If the successful captain from that heavenly contest was to seek new challenges, he could contemplate a fixture against the England side of 1932/33, skippered by Douglas Jardine. Australians would undoubtedly claim that a call would have to be made to 'the other place' to arrange the match, for as England captain during the Bodyline series, Jardine was not held in the greatest of esteem by his opponents.

While he certainly marshalled his team with a sure touch, his generally haughty demeanour, to say nothing of his Harlequins cap, did nothing to endear him to the locals. Leg theory, as it was termed by Jardine rather than the more emotive Bodyline, did the job required in that it won the Ashes for his country, but at a considerable cost in terms of Anglo-Australian relations.

On one occasion, Jardine was fielding near the boundary, oblivious to everything other than the match in progress. He idly flicked away a bothersome fly from his face, only to hear a raucous cry from someone in the crowd. "Hey Jardine. Leave our bloody flies alone."

There is no doubt that captains do make a difference to the performance of a team. Perhaps the greatest example of that came in 1981 when England were playing Australia. Ian Botham was England captain when they lost the first Test and managed a draw in the second. With virtually the same team, Mike Brearley then led them to success in the next three Tests to end the series in possession of the Ashes.

What was the difference between the two men? Botham was a great player while Brearley might have struggled to make the side had he not been such an outstanding leader. A highly intelligent man, he was able to get the best out of those around him, including Botham who had the series of his life after relinquishing the captaincy.

Perhaps the fact that Brearley was not such a gifted player meant that he could empathise with those of his players who were not on a level with a natural cricketing genius like Botham. Whatever the

BELOW Australian captain Steve Waugh talks to his successor Ricky Ponting before retiring on the final day of the fourth Test in Sydney, 6th January 2004

ABOVE Mike Brearley, one of England's great captains, discussing tactics with Ian Botham during the fourth Ashes Test in 1981

towards a draw. Phil Edmonds was bowling his left-arm spin with all the variations he could muster to Jim Love and Richard Lumb who were taking no chances. Just to enliven proceedings, Brearley dispensed with his short leg, but instead of putting the discarded helmet behind the wicket-keeper, he carefully positioned it at short mid-wicket to see whether the prospect of a five-run bonus for hitting it might induce one of the batsmen to play against the spin and get out. The regulations were changed after that so that the helmet has to be placed behind the keeper.

It is also rumoured that on one occasion in Australia, Brearley was trying to slow the game down. Rather than indulging in blatant time-wasting, he took some cake crumbs out after tea and scattered them at the end of the bowler's run-up. Seagulls swooped down to pick up the crumbs as soon as the bowler started to run, the distracted batsman pulled away and valuable time was consumed, as were the crumbs.

difference, Brearley was a natural captaincy genius who was never afraid to try something outrageous if it would help him towards success on the field.

On one occasion, he was leading Middlesex in a county match at Lord's when Yorkshire were batting their way

On the evidence of this and other stories, it might be that there has to be another quality added to the list of those required by great captains. A Machiavellian streak does not go amiss.

Declarations

IT IS THE POSSIBILITY OF BEING able to declare an innings closed that marks cricket out as a game of ultimate sophistication. Whereas most other sports have a set time limit or a requirement to reach a pre-determined score, cricket allows the captain a certain degree of judgement to decide whether he has enough runs, a sufficiently powerful attack or low enough opinion of the opposition to call a halt to his own side's innings and lay down the challenge to his opposite number.

The other captain then has to make a decision as to whether the combination of conditions, the opposition attack and his team's batting strength favours an attempt to score the required runs or play conservatively for a draw. His strategy can change depending on the state of the match at various natural junctions in play as he weighs up the equation, but it all helps to make cricket such a fascinating battle of wits as well as skills. If a captain takes the necessary number of wickets to win the match, his declaration was timed to perfection. If he fails, it is always his fault for batting on too long.

It is only in traditional games of cricket that declarations are possible. It is one of the reasons why purists enjoy the timed form of the game more than limited overs cricket. Having said that, it took a particularly innovative piece of captaincy to have the regulations governing one-day cricket changed to prevent declarations.

ABOVE Brian Rose of Somerset in relaxed mood. His declaration after just one over of their Benson and Hedges match against Worcestershire caused an uproar.

DECLARATIONS

BELOW Graeme Hick hits another run on his way to 98* where he was forced to stop after Michael Atherton's declaration in 1995

Somerset went into the last of their 1979 Benson and Hedges Cup zonal matches at Worcester with nine points from their previous fixtures. Worcestershire had six, as did

BELOW Graeme Hick hits another run on his way to 98* where he was forced to stop after Michael Atherton's declaration in 1995

Glamorgan who were also playing. With three points available for a win, it was possible that wins for Worcestershire and Glamorgan, playing against the unfancied Minor Counties South side, could have lifted both into qualifying positions for the quarter-finals at Somerset's expense. If all three finished on nine points, the rate of wicket-taking would come into play, with Somerset enjoying an advantage over Worcestershire on that basis as they started the match.

With the top two sides from each group qualifying for the next, lucrative stage of the competition, Somerset only needed to keep their strike-rate better than Worcestershire's to be certain of going through. Consequently, after Somerset captain Brian Rose and his opening partner, Peter Denning, had faced one over from Worcestershire's Vanburn Holder, he declared. The only run came from a no ball, but Rose's action denied Worcestershire the opportunity to improve their strike-rate.

It took just ten balls for Worcestershire to score two runs to win and end the match, but start the furore. The hundred or so paying spectators had their money refunded, while the

Test and County Cricket Board (then the governing body of the game in England) voted by 17 to one to disqualify Somerset from the competition for "bringing the game into disrepute". Glamorgan were awarded their place in the quarter-finals. Somerset had not won a major trophy in their history at that point, but by the end of the season they had both the Gillette Cup and the John Player League title in their previously unused trophy cabinet.

Opinions on Rose's decision, which was certainly not all his own, varied from those who damned his actions as being 'not cricket' to others who admired him for exploiting a loophole in the regulations fashioned by the very body that disqualified his county. Whatever the rights and wrongs of the case, the regulations were changed to prevent anyone from declaring in limited-overs cricket in the future.

Where declarations are possible, they can sometimes appear to be cruel on batsmen hoping for personal achievement. Going into the third Test against Australia in 1995, England were two-nil down and needed a win in Sydney to keep their Ashes hopes alive. Graeme Hick had been batting for four and a

quarter hours to reach 98 not out when his captain, Michael Atherton, declared to set Australia 449 to win. They reached 344 for seven by the close.

It might seem a hard decision when Hick was only two short of his century, but Atherton might well have gone on too long as it was. To be fair, rain and bad light seriously limited his options in the field, while Hick blocked three balls in what was going to be the final over of the innings. He never did get a hundred in an Ashes Test.

ABOVE Mark Taylor having declared the Australian innings whilst on 334* against Pakistan in 1998

ABOVE Garry Sobers about to be caught by Colin Cowdrey during the fifth and final Test of the famous declaration series of 1968

Bradman's record. The match was drawn anyway.

Most Test captains will err on the side of caution when it comes to timing their declarations when a series is at stake. Not so Garry Sobers in 1968 at Port of Spain playing against England. Neither side had achieved a victory in a series characterised by some pretty unexciting cricket until the final day of the fourth Test. West Indies began that day on six without loss and enjoying a lead of 122. Sobers batted on until that lead was 214, and declared with eight wickets in hand and 165 minutes of play remaining.

Australian captain Mark Taylor declared against Pakistan in Peshawar on the 1998/99 tour when he was on 334 not out at the close of the second day. It might be thought that was enough for anyone and the time was right to declare. However, his personal score was level with the highest innings by an Australian batsman in Test cricket, and Taylor would not bat on the next day merely to go past Sir Donald

England won by seven wickets and clung on in the fifth Test in Guyana to take the series. Sobers was pilloried in the West Indies for declaring when he did to the extent that for years afterwards, whenever he went through a Caribbean airport, there would be some customs officer who would delight in inquiring of him, "Anything to declare?"

Extras

THERE WAS SOMETHING PARTICU-
larly bruising, at Trent Bridge in 2001,
about the delivery of a no ball sealing
the outcome of the Ashes series against
Australia. Andrew Caddick was the cul-
prit, although in truth he merely
applied a marginal tweak to Australia's
already rampant domination of that
series. It was barely halfway through, yet
Australia had outplayed England so
convincingly that they were doing a lap
of honour with the crystal urn on the
third afternoon of the third Test.

It is quite rare, though, for an extra to
be such a high-profile catalyst. Generally
they are merely irritants to the bowler,
wicket-keeper or fielder, while for the
batsman they are a small but welcome
boost to the running total. Of the four
types of extra (byes, leg byes, wides and
no balls), it is the last that takes up by far
the most space in the laws of the game.

There are all sorts of reasons for calling a no ball, the most straightforward of
which is if the batsman changes his
mode of delivery (right arm to left, or
over the wicket to round) without warning the umpire. And no repeat is now
possible of the grubber bowled by
Australia's Trevor Chappell at Melbourne
in 1981, on the instructions of his captain

ABOVE Damien Martyn
of Australia celebrates in
front of Andrew Caddick
whose no ball in the
third Test confirmed the
retention of the Ashes
by Australia in 2001

ABOVE Derek Pringle, a frequent overstepping offender, prepares to bowl for Essex

and brother Greg, to Brian McKechnie, who was denied the chance to hit the last ball of the match for the six runs New Zealand needed for victory. McKechnie threw his bat away in disgust; underarm bowling is no longer permitted except by special agreement before the match.

The most sensitive section in the no ball law relates to throwing (dealt with in greater depth under T). By far the most common cause, though, is the bowler overstepping. As Law 24 (5) states: 'For a delivery to be fair in respect of the feet, in the delivery stride (i) the bowler's back foot must land within and not touching the return crease. (ii) the bowler's front foot must land with some part of the foot, whether grounded or raised, behind the popping crease.' Bob Willis and Derek Pringle were both regular offenders of the modern era; television viewers may recall Jim Laker's lugubrious "yet another no ball!" as the Essex all-rounder overstepped once more.

Other reasons for calling no ball crop up less frequently, for example, if the ball comes to rest in front of the line of the striker's wicket, without having touched him or his bat. Or if other laws have been broken, relating to the positions of the wicket-keeper or fielders, or dangerous and unfair bowling. Whatever the cause, an extra ball will be added to the over, and the batsman cannot be dismissed unless he is run out or, massively less likely, handles the ball, hits it twice or obstructs the field.

One of the acid tests of a wicket-keeper's competence is the number of byes he concedes. Returning to the laws: 'If the ball, not being a No ball or a Wide, passes the striker without touching his bat or person, any runs completed by the batsmen or a boundary allowance shall be credited as Byes to the batting side.'

One of the great cricket stories concerns the fine Kent wicket-keeper WHV "Hopper" Levett, who found it rather difficult even to get on to the field one morning after a good night out. Legend has it that the first ball flashed past his left ear for four byes,

BELOW The Kent side of 1936 featuring WHV "Hopper" Levett standing third from the left

Many is the time that a wicket-keeper has felt personally affronted as byes are signalled when in his view, the ball would more appropriately have been called wide. If, however, the ball touches the batsman while he is attempting a stroke or trying to avoid it, it becomes a leg bye and the keeper, in scorebook at least, is exonerated. Law 26 (2) states: "If a ball delivered by the bowler first strikes the person of the striker, runs shall be scored only if the umpire is satisfied that the striker has either (i) attempted to play the ball with his bat, or (ii) tried to avoid being hit by the ball.' If he is not satisfied on either of these counts, no Leg bye can be scored.

Like a no ball, a wide counts against the bowler and results in an extra ball having to be bowled in the over. A profusion of wides, unlike no balls, can offer quite a comical aspect to the observer, although in the mind of the bowler (and his captain) they will be anything but amusing. The much-adjusted radar of Devon Malcolm has been a feature of recent years, and who would have been in Stephen Harmison's shoes in Australia in 2002, when the Durham paceman bowled

and the second past his right with the same result. From the next delivery the batsman attempted a leg glance, and the diving Levett took a superlative catch. He got up, dusted himself down and said: "Not bad eh, lads, for the first ball of the day?"

seven wides in a row, and eight in an over, in a warm-up match at Lilac Hill?

Law 25 (1) states: 'If the bowler bowls a ball, not being a No ball, the umpire shall adjudge it a Wide if, according to the definition in (b) below, in his opinion the ball passes wide of the striker where he is standing and would also have passed wide of him standing in a normal guard position. (b) The ball will be considered as passing wide of the striker unless it is sufficiently within his reach for him to be able to hit it with his bat by means of a normal cricket stroke.' Interpretation of a wide in one-day cricket is much stricter than in the longer version, but either way the outcome is expensive for the bowler, as any resulting runs also go down as wides.

Two examples, finally, of the frustration extras can cause to the fielding side. In 1926, Tommy Andrews scored 164 for the Australians against Middlesex at Lord's. He was caught off a no ball three times during the innings. And spare a thought for Gloucestershire's Charlie Parker, who would have taken five wickets in five balls, all of them bowled, during his benefit match against Yorkshire at Bristol in 1922. Unfortunately his second delivery was a no ball.

Fielding

WHOEVER BELIEVES THAT CRICKET boils down to a simple contest between batsman and bowler has not completely grasped the game's deeper subtleties. True, it is generally possible to attribute praise to a batsman for an exquisite cover drive, while blaming the bowler in some measure, perhaps for landing the ball on too full a length. Conversely, the bowler may be feted for following three away swingers with the classic "nip backer" to trap his adversary plumb lbw, but should the batsman have been wiser to the possibility?

More often than not, the bowler is going to need help in securing a dismissal. Every fielder knows that there might be an opportunity, however fleeting, to show the flash of brilliance that can change the course of a match. A catch perhaps – routine or brilliant – or less likely, a run out. In the latter case,

the batsman will probably return to the pavilion knowing that his dismissal had nothing to do with the quality of the bowling.

Take the first-ever World Cup final in 1975. One-day cricket was still in its international infancy, and Vivian Richards was not yet that well known outside his native Antigua. Yet it was his brilliance in the field which tripped up

ABOVE Australian fielders crowd the bat as Jason Gillespie bowls. Australia v West Indies, fourth Test, 2000

Australia – not once, but three times - as they were making a fair fist of a challenging run chase. The victims, Alan Turner and the Chappell brothers, were Australia's one, three and four and all going well when they perished.

Fractional hesitation by the batsmen contributed to the first, while the second and third followed slight misfields, or was Richards craftily misleading them?

The middle one, which accounted for Greg Chappell, came from a direct hit with one stump to aim at. Although Australia battled to the bitter end, it was always going to be hard to recover from such setbacks. West Indies ultimately won an excellent match by 17 runs.

Like the legendary Jack Hobbs of England, who ran out no less than 15 batsmen on the 1911-12 tour of

ABOVE Viv Richards runs out Alan Turner during the 1975 World Cup final

Australia, Richards became a star attraction primarily as one of the greatest batsmen to have played the game, but there are others whose predatory prowess in the field was a significant ticket-seller. Two men from southern Africa, Colin Bland and Jonty Rhodes, fit into this category, as does England's Derek Randall.

Bland used to practice his fielding by throwing at a stump in a hockey net, and occasionally demonstrated his skills before play. The "Golden Eagle" may best be remembered for his performance at the Lord's Test in 1965. Having already run out Jim Parks, Bland intervened still more decisively when Ken Barrington, on 91, played wide of mid-on and called for what appeared to be a safe single. Bland swooped to his left from mid-wicket and hit the stumps side-on to run Barrington out. It was arguably the turning point in the entire series, which South Africa won 1-0.

No one who watched Nottinghamshire or England in the 1970s and 80s will forget one of the most animated fielders in the game's history. Known as "Arkle" he appeared to cover the ground of a steeplechaser several times over. He talked to himself incessantly, a trait as disconcerting for the batsmen as it was infuriating for bowlers when he was at the crease. The joy of Derek Randall, to an England supporter at least, stemmed not only from the exuberance with which he played, but also the singular effect that his presence could have on the course of a match.

Two run-outs stand out, first that of the Australian opener Rick McCosker in the Headingley Test of 1977, when he backed up too far, allowing Randall to

strike like lightning on the stumps from extra cover. The match was won, along with the Ashes. Two years later in the World Cup final at Lord's, the great Barbadian Gordon Greenidge fell victim to a similar swoop from mid-wicket after calling for a sharp single. Sadly for Randall and for England, it was the West Indies who held the trophy aloft at the end of the day.

The era dominated by Randall was not without other fielding stars. For the West Indies both Greenidge and, slightly earlier, Clive Lloyd (dubbed the "Big Cat" for his tigerish brilliance) were both fielders who commanded cautious respect. For Australia, Ross Edwards and Paul Sheahan excelled, as did David Gower for England. Most recently, with the proliferation of one-day internationals placing ever-increasing physical demands on the players, the name of Jonty Rhodes has been to the fore.

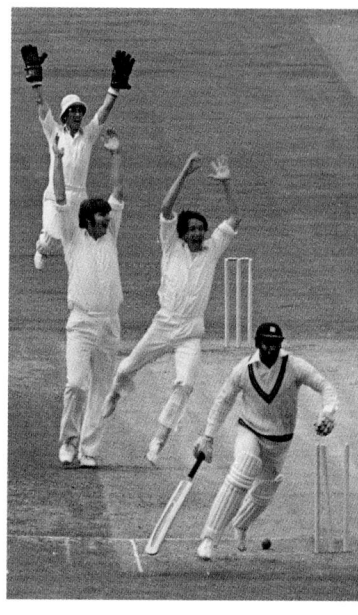

ABOVE Derek Randall runs out Gordon Greenidge in the 1979 World Cup final, Lord's

LEFT Colin Bland, the "Golden Eagle" batting during the memorable Lord's Test of 1965

ABOVE Jonty Rhodes takes a spectacular trademark flying catch to dismiss Robert Croft in August 1998

many spectacular efforts, born out of a rigorous work ethic outside matches as well as in them. When the ball was played to Rhodes, batsmen would think twice before taking a single that would be second nature to virtually any other fielder. Thus he was worth 20-odd runs an innings before he even picked a bat up, and he too excelled in that department of the game.

Rhodes quit first-class cricket at the end of the 2003 season after providing worthy entertainment in a one-off year with Gloucestershire. Fittingly, he completed a run-out in the C&G Final at Lord's to set his team on the path to victory. Shortly after his retirement was announced, he spoke of why fielding was so special to him. "It just stems from the fact that I love being out there," he said. "I'm not an entertainer, I'm not looking to try to impress the people, but I really am having fun. If you're not enjoying it, it can become a bit tedious. But I've loved every minute of it."

Rhodes burst on the scene with a run-out of Randall-like quality in the 1992 World Cup to send back another great batsman in every respect, Pakistan's Inzamam-ul-Haq. It was the first of

So did the spectators. So they always have, and always will, when they witness artistry that adds a wonderfully unpredictable subtlety to the great game of cricket.

Grass

CHESS ON GRASS. This expression refers not to a grandmaster found guilty of smoking illegal substances, but is a means of conveying the complexities of cricket. It is the captain who is moving the pieces at his disposal, while the character of the turf on which the game is played is very often the determining factor in the outcome of a match.

It is not surprising that cricket evolved from a pastime of shepherds on the downlands of south-east England. The grass was kept short by grazing sheep to provide a suitable surface. It is interesting to note that a flock of sheep was kept at Lord's in the early days with the express purpose of mowing the grass. They were confined to a special pen on match days, but, sad to relate, the quality of the outfield they produced would not be acceptable nowadays. In fact, it was not deemed

LORD'S GROUND IN 1837.

acceptable in the middle of the nineteenth century.

In the days before the heavy roller and mowing machines, the actual wicket would be cut using scythes, or even gangs of small boys individually picking off the long stalks of grass. With sheep grazing the outfield, and providing natural, organic fertiliser in abundant quantities, it might be thought that a true surface would be prepared. That is, once the evidence of the sheep had been removed by the ground boys prior to a match. However, John Lillywhite, who played for Sussex and Middlesex at

ABOVE Sheep, the mowers of their day, preparing the Lord's outfield

GRASS

ABOVE A wooden horse-drawn grass roller

the time, reported that Lord's "only resembled a billiard table in one respect and that was in the pockets".

When grounds were developed by owners, such as Thomas Lord, the wickets would be variable at best. It is reported that gravel and other stones were often found on the pitch, as the owner would simply hire casual labour to prepare the ground for matches. One of the first specialist groundsmen was a David Jordan who was rewarded with what was, in 1864, a decent wage of 25 shillings a week by MCC to look after Lord's.

His efforts during a decade of employment were not always appreciated, for when he was replaced by Peter Pearce, a newspaper carried an article that noted how good pitches at Lord's were at one time an exception but, under the care of the new groundsman, "the playing portion of the arena is in faultless condition".

The first machine for mowing the grass was patented in 1830 by Edwin Budding of Stroud. He based his idea on a machine used in the West Country designed to take the nap off cloth. Of course, it was many years after that before motor-driven machinery became available and so horses were used to pull the mowing machines and mass-produced heavy iron rollers, which did not come into use until the 1870s.

To avoid damaging the turf, these horses were fitted with specially designed leather boots. Catalogues of equipment for tending cricket grounds were still featuring horse-drawn machinery up until the outbreak of the Second World War. Some of these animals became characters in their own right. There is a tale that the resident horse at Trent Bridge, on noticing that the particularly inept number eleven batsman was making his way to the wicket, would actually take up his position between the shafts of the roller unaided. The animal knew that it would be but a short interval before it was required for work between innings.

As well as mechanisation, there was an increasing input from the world of science when it came to the preparation of cricket pitches. Long after the sheep had been moved from cricket fields, natural, organic fertilisers were virtually the only ones available. It was often said that the best pitches came from cows. Cowpats were not actually applied to the surface, but they were put into sacks that were in turn soaked for days in tubs of water and occasionally agitated.

The resulting sediment at the bottom of the tub was then applied to the wicket to act as both a top-dressing and a fertiliser in one go. The process produced some wonderful pitches when given time to work and then rolled out, but it did not do to lick your fingers if you were a spin bowler!

The introduction of chemical fertilisers and artificial dressings was frowned upon by the authorities as they became more widely used. In 1901 it was the MCC who contacted all county clubs with a warning that "it is undesirable, in the interests of cricket, that the wickets should be prepared artificially (i.e. in

BELOW Improved mechanisation and science have created beautifully prepared grounds such as Hobart's Bellerive Oval hosting this 2004 match between Australia and Zimbabwe

GRASS

ABOVE Come rain or shine, waterhogs or rollers are at the heart of a groundsman's art as the Lord's (Left) and Oval (Right) grounds-men will attest

any way other than by water and roller)". That could not happen today as chemicals, dressings and all types of processes designed to produce a better underlying structure are used to make a cricket pitch.

Even with these additional aids at his disposal, watering, rolling and mowing are still at the heart of the groundsman's art. Like everything else in cricket, the important thing is balance. It is difficult to get right, especially when the weather can intervene at any moment to tilt it hopelessly out of kilter, while the groundsman can rarely please everyone. It is either too flat for the bowlers or not fair to the batsmen. And nowhere do pitches have the same pace and even

bounce as they used to, if we listen to those who were playing a few years ago, when others no doubt made the same comment.

The only answer would seem to be artificial pitches. In some countries cricket was always played on matting, and practice wickets in nets were often concrete or some other hard surface that bore no relation to conditions in the middle. In recent times, there have been instances of wickets being prepared away from the ground on trays that are then lowered into position using cranes. Furthermore, great advances have been made in producing artificial pitches that look and play like turf but without the need for such specialised maintenance.

They are particularly useful in places where resources or climate do not allow proper turf pitches to be kept up to standard. It is much better to learn to play on a good artificial pitch than a poor turf wicket or net area where nobody will acquire the skills of the game. Artificial pitches also take away the regional variety of cricket. England and New Zealand historically offer green, seaming pitches, Australia, the West Indies and South Africa have been noted for fast, true pitches, while dry, dusty turners can be found on the sub-continent. Pitches are responsible for the character of a country's cricket.

Nowadays, there is even a type of plastic pitch that can be rolled out and put down on football pitches, in car parks, or any piece of open ground where there is room for cricket. The game has been played on ice and on sand, but for proper cricket, there is nothing quite like an immaculately prepared stretch of natural grass.

ABOVE Without an artificial pitch cricketers might struggle for a game in St. Moritz

Headgear

IMAGINE WG GRACE BATTING IN A helmet! It really doesn't bear thinking about, and for many of the game's traditionalists, it was scarcely more bearable when protective headgear did come into the game, nearly a century after WG played his first Test. 'It's unsightly,' they said. 'You can't recognise who's batting. In fact, it's the end of civilisation as we know it.'

A generation after their introduction, helmets have made cricket more civilised rather than less, and such voices are silent. It is still alarming enough watching a batsman being hit on the helmet, as often occurs, but the alarm is mild and tempered by relief that thirty years ago, the outcome could have been so much worse.

One of the catalysts for the introduction of protective headgear was an incident in New Zealand during the

England tour there in 1974/75, Ewen Chatfield, a fast bowler making his Test debut in Auckland, had been batting stubbornly at number 11 when he was hit on the temple by a ball from the Lancashire fast bowler Peter Lever. His heart stopped and he swallowed his tongue. After the England physiothera-

concerned. With hindsight, it is astonishing that the Bodyline tour of 1932/3, in which a number of Australian batsmen were hit and injured, did not precipitate the introduction of helmets. Heaven knows what might have happened if the sustained barrage put up by the West Indies in the 1980s had been aimed at helmetless heads.

Until the late 1970s helmets were barely seen, although the first recorded example of head protection can be found a century earlier, when one was used by Nottinghamshire's Richard Daft. In India in the 1920s, pith helmets were worn for protection from the sun.

OPPOSITE Helmets are now de rigueur as Shane Warne and Daniel Vettori show during the 2005 Tsunami Appeal match between the ICC Rest of the World XI and the Asian XI

BELOW Makhaya Ntini of South Africa is hit on the helmet by a ball from Brett Lee of Australia in 2001

pist Bernard Thomas had provided mouth-to-mouth resuscitation and heart massage, Chatfield was taken to hospital, and mercifully he regained consciousness an hour later.

The incident was by no means the first to illustrate the dangers of cricket, particularly where fast bowling was

than leaving Dodds poleaxed as Trueman certainly anticipated.

Their wider arrival was initially gradual. Mike Brearley, when England captain, wore a skull cap, which protected his temples as well as his head, beneath his cap in the 1977 Ashes series, and less than a year later crash helmets were worn for the first time in Test cricket, in the series between West Indies and Australia. The broad outline of present-day helmets soon followed, and by the early 1980s they were worn almost universally against faster bowling, although there were some notable exceptions. The great Viv Richards spurned them, continuing to sport the famous maroon West Indies cap. And Ian Chappell simply couldn't bear to wear a helmet against the Poms, although his career was nearing its end when they came in anyway.

To be fair to those aforementioned traditional voices, helmets have deprived the game of a certain aesthetic value, as is evident from video and photographs of yesteryear. But the time-honoured caps are still often seen in the field, as well as on batsmen when spinners are operating at both ends. The sunhat is also a regular feature, its rim now rather broader than when Phil Edmonds was

Patsy Hendren, of Middlesex and England, stitched two extra peaks onto his cap to protect his temples in 1933, while Dickie Dodds, an Essex opening batsman in the 1950s, wore part of a riding helmet under his cap, and it once proved very effective when he was facing Fred Trueman. The ball hit him on the head, and to the bowler's amazement ricocheted for four leg byes, rather wearing something akin to an inverted flowerpot in the early 1980s. So are sunglasses and even light enhancers.

Test caps, of course, have remained distinctive and largely unchanged over the years. The England cap is one of the easiest to spot – navy blue, with three white lions royally crowned. The lions stand out more today than ever before, but the basic design has remained largely unchanged over half a century. So too the baggy green of Australia, adorned by a kangaroo and an emu. The silver fern stands out proudly against the black of the New Zealand cap, while a yellow star shines on Pakistan's green. The West Indies maroon is particularly attractive, with its badge depicting the sun, sea and a Caribbean island, upon which stand the wicket and a palm tree.

Old photographs and paintings of the game reveal how styles of headgear have developed over the years. In an etching that depicts a cricket match on the famous field near White Conduit House in 1787, the players are wearing wigs, which presumably provided a degree of protection as well as fashionable elegance. However, caps with a fair resemblance to those worn today are evident

ABOVE Glenn McGrath sporting the traditional Australian Baggy Green

in an earlier painting by Francis Hayman of "Cricket in Mary-le-bone Fields" completed in 1744. More than a century later William Clark, creator of the All-England XI in 1846, appears resplendent in a top hat. Bowler hats were worn in the 1860s, and caricatures drawn in 1872 show the secretary of the Marylebone Cricket Club, RA Fitzgerald, wearing a "pillbox" MCC cap without a peak, while upon the head of WG Grace rests the authentic precursor of the modern peaked cap.

By 1900 it was becoming the norm,

ABOVE Cricket being played at White Conduit House, Islington, in 1787

RIGHT Andrew Strauss shows the value of a helmet during the 2004 Lord's Test against New Zealand

although standard England caps were not always worn in Tests during the following century. Douglas Jardine famously wore his Harlequins cap even when he was captaining England. Many players between his time and the late 1970s are pictured batting bare-headed, something of a rarity now. Heaven knows what Jardine and his contemporaries would have made of the headgear, indeed the entire kit that is currently worn in one-day internationals. And who would have imagined wicket-keepers wearing helmets until just a few years ago? It is commonplace for them to do so now when standing up, and it makes sense, given the potential danger of the hustle and bustle in this form of cricket.

Research into headgear safety is continuing and expensive. The international headgear company Albion spent £800,000 developing its top-of-the range helmet, which is worn by, amongst many others, Andrew Strauss, Justin Langer and Adam Gilchrist. A century from now, perhaps someone will have come up with a still more lightweight and sartorially elegant version of the helmets that currently dominate the game. But it is impossible to imagine a return to the flimsy protection donned by batsmen of yesteryear. The kit in which cricket is played will doubtless evolve for as long as the game itself.

International Cricket Council

THE TROUBLE WITH CRICKET IS that it requires such a specialised surface on which to play. A football pitch can double up as a rugby pitch, athletes can perform virtually anywhere and baseball can be played wherever there is room to put down four sacks, without needing to worry unduly about the quality of the surface.

It was for that very reason that baseball took over from cricket as the major sport of North America. Up until the Civil War, which broke out in 1861, cricket held sway while baseball was considered to be a children's game. Then came the war and for four years it was difficult to get equipment and impossible to get properly prepared pitches on

which to play. The troops needed athletic entertainment, and so the four sacks were thrown down, a bat and a ball produced, and the soldiers went back from the conflict hooked into baseball.

It should also be remembered that the first international match to be played took place in 1844. It was not Australia versus England (that first appeared on

ABOVE The 1859 England touring party to America. Back row (from left to right): Carpenter, Caflyn, Lockyer, Wisden (seated), Stephenson, G Parr, Grundy, Cesar, Hayward and Jackson. Seated at front: Diver (left) and John Lillywhite

the fixture list in 1877) but Canada against the United States. If it seems strange that such nations should feature so prominently in cricket's past, the International Cricket Council has a policy of spreading the great game so that such nations might well feature prominently in the future.

The ICC is the game's governing body as far as international cricket is concerned. It began life as the Imperial Cricket Conference on June 15th 1909 when representatives from England, Australia and South Africa met at Lord's. India, New Zealand and the West Indies joined in 1926 and, by 1953, Pakistan were elected to join and membership of the 'club' rose to seven.

It was not until 1981 that Sri Lanka achieved membership, but by then South Africa had left the Commonwealth (in 1961) and was not re-admitted to the ICC fold until 1991. A year later, Zimbabwe were admitted, as were Bangladesh in 2000. As full members, these countries could play Test cricket.

The organisation changed its name in 1965 to become the International Cricket Conference, reflecting a change in political attitudes that found the word 'imperial' unacceptable, and passed a resolution that allowed membership from outside the Commonwealth. It was 1989 that saw the most recent name change to International Cricket Council rather than Conference, as it was now to be less of a forum for discussion and more a proper governing body in every sense.

Once the Commonwealth restriction was lifted, other categories of membership were introduced. Associate Members, of which there are currently 27, come just below Full Members in the pecking order. They are the cricket-playing countries where the game is well established and organised in a way that meets certain ICC criteria.

Affiliate Members come a little further down the order. The criteria for membership are not as rigorous as for Associates, but these 55 nations still have to comply with regulations covering the governance of the game within their territories. Those that do not fall into yet another category of Prospective Members. Here, in what might appear some pretty unlikely places, there is some sort of organised cricket, but not yet with the degree of sophistication or reach to justify the 'Affiliate' tag.

With the amount of development work going in such countries, it might not be long before they too will be pressing for elevation. It is in this way that the ICC is pursuing one of the objectives contained in its mission statement, whereby its aims include: "promoting the game as a global sport, protecting the spirit of cricket and optimising commercial opportunities for the benefit of the game".

It might be relatively easy to achieve all of those objectives in isolation; to deliver all three at the same time presents problems of a major magnitude. As the commercial opportunities expand and the ICC finds itself at the head of an international business operation, so too does the greed and political manoeuvring. The spirit of cricket can sometimes take second place to commercial ambitions, while the promotion of the game as a global sport can increase the possibilities of it all going horribly wrong and spiralling out of control.

The ICC is itself at a critical stage of development. It is large enough to be the object of power struggles but small enough to be vulnerable to those who might want to use it for their own ends. It is, however, making rapid strides to get to a position where it can defeat its enemies and establish itself as the

BELOW Children playing cricket with a stick and a coke can in South Africa

ABOVE The First Battalion Royal Welsh Fusiliers XI in 1888, sowing seeds of the game during service in India

RIGHT Former Indian cricketer and ICC coach Vinod Sharma gives batting instruction during a cricket coaching camp at the Karnali Singh Stadium, New Delhi 2003

governing body of a global sport.

Cricket might not yet have that universal appeal of association football, but its five development regions work with a missionary zeal to spread the word. ICC is trying to ensure that countries from Argentina to Zambia appreciate what the game has to offer, and why it is being played so widely.

In the early days, it was often spread by the Army and Royal Navy as they campaigned around the globe. As British rule was established, cricket took root at the same time. Now there is a reverse colonisation. Visit any emerging cricket nation and you will find that the heartbeat of cricket is maintained by ex-patriots from major cricketing countries, and very often a majority of players come from the Asian community.

The game was taken to them, and their passion for it is helping the ICC to spread it into new areas. So successfully are they doing it that local government officers in some very unlikely places are suddenly faced with demands for cricket pitches. In Norway the demand for the game is such that national television has agreed to show live cricket and highlights packages.

In places like that, with a harsh climate preventing the development of turf pitches, modern technology has come to the game's aid. Artificial pitches that play like turf can be installed or, in even more remote venues, plastic pitches can be laid on virtually any surface to provide facilities for cricket. If only they had been available in North America in the 1860s.

Jaffa

IF CONTESTANTS ON ONE OF THOSE television quiz shows had to determine the true definition of the word 'jaffa', they could have problems. They could be offered: "Jaffa; a port city in the Middle East", "jaffa; a sweet variety of orange", or "jaffa; a particularly good ball bowled in cricket". All are true, and all are related. Jaffa oranges originate from the area around Jaffa, while a ball that the bowler considers to be sweet and juicy is worthy of carrying the name.

Quite when the term was first used in cricket is lost in time, but it is one of those that, once coined, has assumed an enduring place in the game's lexicon. It is evocative enough to be used by cricketers in that particular way of theirs when they cannot bring themselves to use plain language to describe something out of the ordinary. To be fair, there are occasions when the delivery might not merit the description but it is still employed. However, there are other times when a particular ball is of such perfection that it can only merit one description. It was an absolute jaffa!

One such came at Old Trafford in 1993. There could be no doubt that it was a jaffa, because it was labelled the "ball of the century" and few could name other contenders. It was Shane Warne's first ball in Ashes cricket, bowled to Mike Gatting, and since described by

ABOVE Shane Warne comes in to bowl his first ball in Ashes cricket

ABOVE Gatting aghast as he is bowled by that ball from Shane Warne

the bowler as "a complete fluke". In case a reminder is needed, it turned from outside Gatting's legs with enough vigour to leave the England captain not just out but utterly nonplussed, bowled off-stump. "The first couple of balls you bowl are just warm-ups, and you just hope to get them somewhere near the right spot," said Warne. "To bowl the perfect leg-break first up – I think it was just meant to be."

The thing about the Warne ball was that it occupied a place of such significance, not only in the innings and the match, but also in the series as a whole. Gatting was known to be a good player of spin and had the experience to counter Warne. At the same time, Warne had not established himself as the complete leg-spinner in English conditions before the Test began. One ball into his first spell, and Warne had become a legend.

It was at Lord's in 1999 that Chris Read, playing in only his second Test,

was the victim of another genuine jaffa. It might well have done for many a batsman of greater accomplishment than Read, which was perhaps unfortunate for the bowler, Chris Cairns of New Zealand, for it was perfectly delivered and had exactly the effect that he was seeking.

Cairns, a genuine all-rounder, could bowl at a very acceptable pace when at his fittest and he was enjoying the conditions in England, where the ball was responding when he tried to move it either in the air or off the pitch. In this instance, he did not try to do either, but bowled a huge, looping slower ball coming out the back of his hand.

Batsmen get into a pattern of watching the ball from the hand and expecting it to go along roughly the same trajectory. This one was on a different plane and at a different pace, causing Read to lose sight of it completely. Instinctively, he ducked down, only to find that the ball floated on a gentle parabola to bowl him. Cairns was justifiably jubilant while Read trudged back to the pavilion having been made to look rather foolish.

It is one thing to produce a magic ball like a conjurer, but quite another to bowl a succession of them. A bunch of jaffas tends to take the spotlight off a particular ball, but if a bowler can string together a succession of them, he is marked out as one of the game's greats. That label could certainly be applied to West Indian fast bowler Michael Holding.

Known as "whispering death" for his ability to glide over the turf in his run up before delivering a ball with deadly intent, Holding has to his credit one of the most memorable overs bowled in Test cricket. Everyone remembers it with awe, none more so than England batsman Geoff Boycott who had the misfortune to be on the receiving end.

It was in 1981 at the Kensington Oval in Bridgetown, Barbados, that Holding

summoned up such pace and perfect accuracy that even as good and experienced batsman as Boycott had no answer to it. Holding responded to the atmosphere to bowl five balls of such fearsome intent that the batsman did well to survive. The sixth was the sweetest of jaffas, uprooting Boycott's off stump. Furthermore, Holding repeated the trick when Ian Botham threatened to claw back the initiative later in England's innings. Clive Lloyd called up him up again and he mustered equal fury to have Botham caught behind.

At the Oval in 1976, the pitch had been specially prepared to draw Holding's fire, and that of his fellow

ABOVE Chris Cairns celebrates taking the wicket of a stupefied Chris Read with a classic slower ball, Lord's 1999

LEFT Michael Holding bowls Alan Knott to take his fourteenth wicket of the fifth Test at The Oval, August 1976

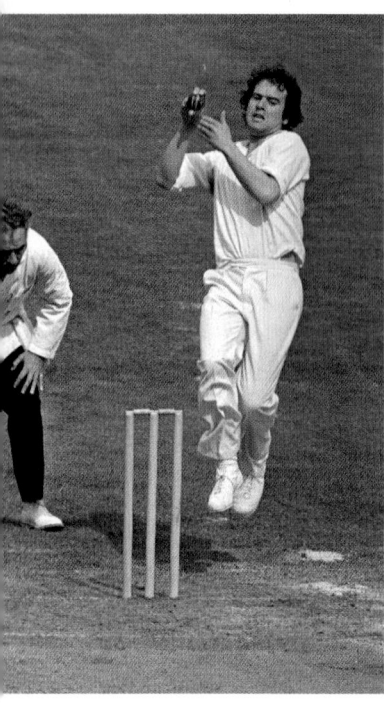

fast bowlers. The ploy worked to an extent. The other members of the West Indian pace quartet were relatively ineffective. Holding was inspired. Eight for 92 in the first innings was followed by six for 57 in the second in a fast bowling performance, on a totally unhelpful pitch, to rank alongside any the world has seen.

It is not often that a batsman presents a jaffa to a bowler, but there was a time when a recent chief executive of the England and Wales Cricket Board, Tim Lamb, was a medium fast bowler with Northamptonshire. Despite the fact that there were some fearsome new ball attacks around in county cricket at the time, the unlikely combination of Lamb and Jim Griffiths could claim a better record than any of their more vaunted colleagues when it came to claiming the wicket of one of England's great Test batsmen, David Gower.

The prospect of a visit to Wantage Road to play Northamptonshire should not have struck fear into the heart of a batsman of Gower's class, but time and time again he fell to one of the opening pair, and usually Lamb. In recognition of the fact, and taking account of the expression "he could roll him over with an orange", Gower paused in the middle while coming in to bat for Leicestershire, looked around to see Lamb fielding at fine leg, and promptly rolled an orange along the ground towards him, calling: "Get me out with that then!"

There was another occasion when an unnamed bowler was playing in an early-season televised match in the John Player League. The umpire called play and, as the cameras closed in on the bowler running in to bowl the first ball of the new season, he released not the ball but an orange. It was of a full length, enticing the batsman to drive, which he did with the expected messy and explosive result. It might have been the start of the expression 'bowling a jaffa'. Or could it simply have been a case of the bowler taking the pith?

Knights

NO FEWER THAN 16 TEST CRICKETERS have achieved the honour of being knighted for their services to the game. Seven represented England, six played for the West Indies, while of the remaining three, one captained India, another, an Australian, was the greatest batsman of them all, and the third was surely the finest bowler to play for New Zealand.

If Don Bradman was the greatest batsman, there is also no doubt about who was the most prolific. Jack Hobbs, of Surrey and England, ended his career with a monumental 61,237 first-class runs and 197 centuries. Knighted in 1953, he was known as "The Master", playing first-class cricket for more than 30 years and, astonishing to imagine today, scoring 98 of his hundreds after reaching the age of 40. Also knighted in 1953 was the amateur HDG "Shrimp"

Leveson-Gower, who led England in South Africa in 1909/10.

Another amateur, the Rajkumar of Vizianagram, better known as "Vizzy", led India in three Tests in England in 1936. Although his achievements on the field could respectfully be described as modest, he nonetheless received his knighthood during the tour. A year later, another knighthood was bestowed on a cricketer who gave an unsurpassed variety of service to the game in England. Pelham Warner played in 15 Tests, captained England in Australia, later served as a selector, was founder editor of The Cricketer magazine, and wrote or edited some 20 cricket books.

A Test average of 99.94 speaks for itself, although it is impossible to resist

ABOVE Jack Hobbs batting for Surrey in 1926

BELOW The Rajkumar of Vizianagram relaxes during India's 1936 tour of England

any other produced by England. Scorer of what was then a world record 364 at The Oval against Australia in 1938, Len Hutton was also the first professional to captain England, and scored 129 first-class centuries. All that, without six war years in which he sustained an injury that left his left arm two inches shorter than his right. Apart from everything else he achieved, his two Ashes victories in 1953 and 1954/55 no doubt contributed as much as anything to him receiving a knighthood.

The emergence of the West Indies in the mid-20th century owes incalculably to the "Three Ws" from Barbados. The youngest, Clyde Walcott, was also physically the most imposing. His great series were against England in 1953/54, in which he scored 698 runs, and above all against Australia in 1955, when he scored 827 runs against the likes of Lindwall, Miller and Benaud. He was eventually knighted in 1994, a year before Everton Weekes, whose pursuit of big hundreds was at times reminiscent of Bradman and whose eventual Test average – 58 from 48 – was the best of the three.

But it was Frank Worrell who was generally regarded as the most elegant.

the much-told story of Don Bradman's last innings at The Oval in 1948 when, needing just four to take his Test career average past the hundred mark, he was bowled second ball for a duck. He was knighted the following year. Of his 29 Test hundreds in 80 innings, the 309 he made in a day at Headingley was perhaps the most memorable. Suffice to say that in the 1930s and 40s his domination of the game was total. As a later great Australian, Steve Waugh, put it after Bradman died in 2001: "If he dominated his era, I think it's fair to say he'd dominate any era, including ours, to a similar degree. A genius is a genius."

Three years after Hobbs was knighted, the same honour was bestowed on a batsman who perhaps bears comparison with him more than

Stylish and orthodox with a deft late cut, he was never seen to hit across the line. He became one of the West Indies' great captains, once and for all exploding the myth in the Caribbean that a coloured player was not fit to lead a team. Transcending the regional rivalries between the dispersed islands, he turned the West Indies into a team to take on the world, laying the foundations for their 1980s invincibility. Knighted in 1964, he tragically died of leukaemia three years later aged just 42.

Worrell's successor as West Indies captain, Garry Sobers, was the greatest all-rounder of them all. In versatility he was unique. Good enough for a Test

place as a dashing left-handed batsman alone, he was a penetrative new ball bowler who could also turn to spin, orthodox or not, and a supreme fielder close to the wicket. He it was who broke Hutton's world batting record, with 365 against Pakistan, and in that legendary over at Swansea, deposited the hapless Malcolm Nash for six sixes in an over. The Queen dubbed Sobers a knight in his native Barbados in 1975. His contemporary in the West Indies side of the 1960s, the opening batsman Conrad Hunte, was also knighted in 1998, as much for the charity work he undertook after retirement as for his exploits in the game.

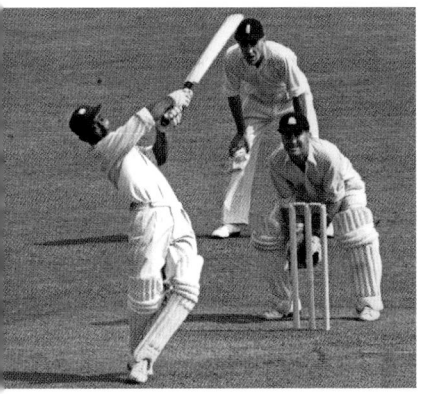

ABOVE Garry Sobers cuts one to the boundary during the 1973 Lord's Test

LEFT Frank Worrell taking on the English bowling at Trent Bridge, 1950

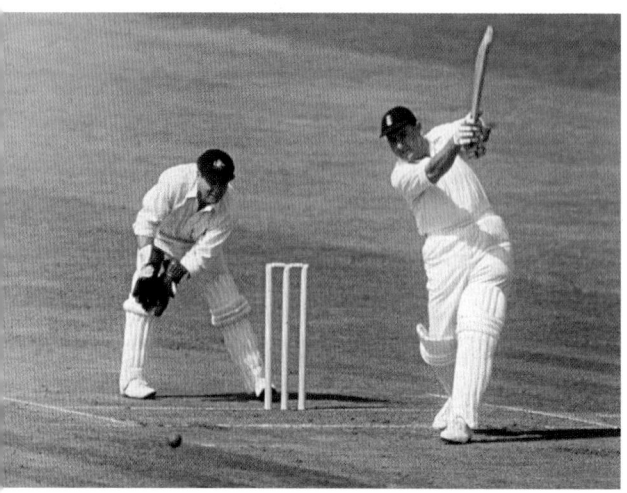

ABOVE Colin Cowdrey takes on the Australians at The Oval in 1968

and Thompson, would be hard to better. Cowdrey was later elevated to the peerage as Baron Cowdrey of Tonbridge.

In 1990, Richard Hadlee achieved the rarity of a knighthood while still playing Test cricket, appropriately enough on his last tour of England. Such was his consistency that it seemed almost inevitable that he would celebrate the achievement with the 36th five-wicket haul of his career in his final game, at Edgbaston that same summer. His mastery of pace, swing and seam was born out of utter dedication to hard work and season-by-season targets, and aggressive batting added to his inestimable value to New Zealand.

The man described by Bradman as the most difficult bowler he batted against in certain conditions is also England's most recent knight. Alec Bedser, bastion of Surrey and England, joined Hadlee on the list in 1997 in a recent and possibly belated tilt towards bowling skills. A peerless bowler of in swing and late cut, he was also chairman of the England selectors for 12 years.

In 1986 Gubby Allen, fast bowler, dependable batsman, England captain and chairman of selectors, became the next English knight. Colin Cowdrey, like Worrell a study in elegance when batting, followed in 1992. Of many memorable Test innings, Cowdrey's 154 at Headingley 1957, when he added 411 with Peter May to deprive West Indies of an apparently certain victory, perhaps stands out. And as an exercise in bravery, his decision to fly to Australia at short notice in 1974/75 to bolster England's buckling batting against Lillee

The most recent knighthood rests with the one Antiguan to be so honoured, surely the most awesome batsman of his generation. Vivian Richards, whose swaggering gait alone as he approached the crease was enough to strike fear into the heart of the bowler. The better the bowler, the more determined Richards was to dominate, unflinchingly sporting the maroon West Indies cap in the age of the helmet. Try though bowlers might to contain him by adjusting their line, it usually ended in heartbreak as Richards, hawk-eyed and muscular, improvised to send the ball skimming where it simply had no right to go.

Others who have adorned the game in different capacities include the great Trinidadian all-rounder Learie Constantine. He was later knighted primarily for his services as a barrister, politician and diplomat. The noted actor Aubrey Smith, who led England in his one Test in South Africa in 1889, was knighted for services to Anglo-American amity 55 years later. The earliest knighted Englishmen closely connected with the game, Francis Lacey and Frederick Toone, received the honour primarily for their service as administrators, and of course Neville Cardus, admired by all lovers of cricket literature, was knighted for services to cricket and music journalism.

ABOVE Richard Hadlee appeals for the wicket of Graham Gooch at The Oval, 1990, the year he was knighted

LEFT Viv Richards - one of the most awesome batsmen of them all

LBW

IT ALL APPEARS SO SIMPLE. The expression 'leg before wicket' suggests that if the leg gets in the way of the ball hitting the stumps, the batsman is out, yet it becomes more complex than that. That is why the LBW Law causes more argument and discussion than any of the other 41 Laws of Cricket as determined by the MCC.

That august body sets it out in black and white in Law 36 (Leg before wicket):

"The striker is out LBW in the circumstances set out below.

(a) The bowler delivers a ball, not being a No ball

and (b) the ball, if it is not intercepted full pitch, pitches in line between wicket and wicket or on the off side of the striker's wicket

and (c) the ball not having previously touched his bat, the striker intercepts the ball, either full pitch or after pitching, with any part of his person

and (d) the point of impact, even if above the level of the bails

either (i) is between wicket and wicket

or (ii) is either between wicket and wicket or outside the line of the off stump, if the striker has made no genuine attempt to play the ball with his bat

and (e) but for the interception, the ball would have hit the wicket."

In plain language, the batsman is out if the umpire can be satisfied that a legal delivery striking the batsman on the pad did not pitch outside the leg stump and would have gone on to hit the wicket. That is providing it did not make contact with the bat before the pad and, if it strikes the pad outside the line of off stump, the batsman was making no effort to play the ball.

Is that language plain enough? Probably not, but that is exactly why Law 36 becomes such a contentious area. As soon as you take the opinion of a human being into the equation, you have grounds for debate. This is because you have at least two other human beings a) who will not be totally convinced that the umpire deserves to be included in the term "human race" and b) whose day, match, season and entire life could revolve around this one decision.

For every batsman who thinks that a) it pitched outside leg and/or b) he got an edge and/or c) it would not have hit another set, there is a bowler who is equally convinced that it would have knocked all three stumps out of the ground. If the umpire turns down the appeal, he is likely to be subjected to sarcastic questions from the bowler like: "How was that missing? Was it going under?" or, "What was that missing, then? Middle stump?"

Before 1744, there would have been no grounds for such banter, as there was no such thing as leg before wicket. The batsman could simply kick the ball away with impunity, except for a lingering pain in his shin, as pads were not worn in those days. In that year, however, an embryonic lbw regulation emerged as

OPPOSITE
A passionate LBW appeal by Brett Lee against India, 2003

LEFT That's out! Umpire Steve Bucknor raises his finger as Shane Warne takes the wicket of Akram Khan of Bangladesh for a duck in 1999

umpires were empowered to prevent a batsman "standing unfair to the strike".

The law really took shape in 1774 when a batsman could be given out "if he puts his leg before the wicket with a design to stop the ball from hitting the wicket". As the legislation of the game advanced at pace, an amendment appeared in 1788 which demanded that for an lbw decision to be possible, the ball had to pitch between wicket and wicket and to be going on to hit the stumps, but the clause covering the batsman's intent was omitted.

The bowlers found that the balance swung in their favour in 1929 when there was an experiment to allow the batsman to be given out even if the ball hit the bat on its way to the pad and everything else allowed the decision to be given. What many people, virtually all of them bowlers, think to be a sensible

idea lasted only until 1933.

It was in 1937 that the first major change to the 1788 law took place. There was a two-year experiment before it was deemed that a batsman could be out lbw to a ball pitching outside the off stump, providing it struck the pad between wicket and wicket.

In practice, this meant that it was only when going back that a batsman could be given out lbw to a ball pitching outside the off stump. If he went forward and he was hit on the pad in front of the wicket by a ball pitching outside off stump, it would almost certainly be going down the leg side. So, batsman soon learned that they could go forward and kick it away in safety.

This was not edifying as a spectacle, yet it had become such a widespread strategy that yet another experimental

ruling was introduced in 1970 whereby the old 1774 intent clause came back into play. A batsman could be given out lbw even if the point at which the ball struck the pad was outside the line of off stump, if he made no attempt to play the ball. Considered a success, the experiment was accepted officially in 1972 and included in the MCC's Laws of Cricket 1980 version.

Essentially, in three stages over two hundred years, cricket had moved from asking the umpires to judge whether the batsman was "standing unfair to strike" to the current situation whereby he has to answer other questions requiring keen judgement. Did the ball pitch outside leg stump? Was it going to hit the stumps? Did the ball touch the bat? And, for the first time since 1788, if the ball made contact with the pad outside off stump, was the batsman playing a stroke at the ball?

Upon the umpire's instant decision can the outcome of a cricket match sometimes depend. There can be other consequences as well, with the aforementioned impact on the day, season and entire life, but if the official had to consider those as well, there would be few willing to do the job.

Match-fixing

ON THE 19TH JUNE 1998, UNDER blue skies in London NW8, Lord's was the only place for a cricket lover to be. South Africa, on their second tour of England since re-admission to the ICC, were rebuilding their innings after early difficulties with Dominic Cork. Their captain, Hansie Cronje, and star fielder Jonty Rhodes were forging an entertaining partnership of 184 that enabled the tourists to surge back into the match.

It was Test cricket at its best, the magnificent, sunlit old ground studded with attractive strokeplay. Too bad that the initiative England had gained on the first morning was being wrested away from them; this was top class, competitive cricket, fairly played and amiably observed by the grey-headed MCC members perched on their tall chairs in the Long Room. When Rhodes was out shortly after reaching his hundred, they stood as one to applaud him as he returned through that hallowed hall.

Cronje had matched Rhodes stroke for stroke, and although he fell 19 short of a century, his reputation was near its zenith. Here was a God-fearing cricketer of considerable talent, touted (if the word is appropriate in this context) for some years as his country's captain before the retirement of his predecessor,

Kepler Wessels. He had the full respect of his team and his opponents, and was playing an influential part in what was to be a convincing win at the "Cathedral of Cricket". All, it seemed, was well with the world.

Tragically for Cronje, and for the game that he and countless others dragged through the mire, it was less than two years before the world was shocked to an unprecedented degree to discover otherwise. On the 7th April 2000, it was claimed by the Delhi police in India that they had recorded mobile phone calls between Cronje and a member of an illegal betting syndicate. Charges followed of criminal conspiracy relating to rigging matches and betting. Cronje denied any wrongdoing, and such was his standing that he was widely believed.

The moment four days later, when he decided to come clean, was a watershed in cricket's history. Quite apart from finishing Cronje as a cricketer, it set a chain of events in motion that led to substantial fines for some players, and lifetime bans for two of them. It placed under a dazzling public spotlight claims, hitherto hazily shrouded, that were later described by Lord Condon,

who headed the Anti-Corruption Unit set up by the ICC, as "the tip of the iceberg".

It may never be known where this peculiarly malevolent species of ivy sank its roots, or how intricately it spread, indeed still spreads, its tendrils. Undoubtedly the explosion of one-day international fixtures, with venues added to the list as far afield as Sharjah, Singapore and Toronto, was a factor. The potential for betting on cricket had been grasped by a Delhi bank clerk, Mukesh Kumar Gupta (alias "John" or "MK"), as far back as the mid-1980s, and a decade later he was performing on a crowded and massively lucrative stage. Asia, where match fixing was known to be an issue well before Cronje's involvement surfaced, was his heartland.

The allegations made by Shane Warne, Mark Waugh and Tim May in 1994 against the Pakistan captain, Salim Malik, had already prompted an

ABOVE From Hero to Zero. How the South African newspapers reacted to Cronje's admission that he received illegal sums of money.

OPPOSITE Hansie Cronje batting at Lord's, June 1998

However it was Cronje's actions, entrapment, denial and subsequent confession that were the catalyst for the King Commission in South Africa, the Central Bureau of Investigation's report in India, and the ICC's Anti-Corruption Unit.

Staggeringly, it emerged at the King Commission that the entire South African team had considered an offer to throw a one-day match in 1996. The CBI report led to the admission by the former Indian captain, Mohammad Azharuddin, that he had been involved in fixing matches. Like Malik, he was banned for life, left immortally and tantalisingly poised one short of a hundred Test caps. It detailed a series of meetings that Gupta claimed to have held with high-profile cricketers from all over the world. England's Alec Stewart was one who denied ever knowingly meeting Gupta and was subsequently cleared of any wrongdoing.

But the bigger picture emerging from the separate inquiries was a far from pretty one. Players under-performing, information bought, new cars presented. Like a virulent flea Gupta hopped from one cricketer to another, and in 1996 he achieved, through Azharuddin, an introduction to Cronje,

enquiry in Pakistan. That eventually led to the Qayyum report, which triggered a life ban on Malik. In the meantime Waugh and Warne were both fined for receiving money from an Indian bookmaker in exchange for information.

a match" of the rain-ruined fifth Test against England at Centurion Park.

Soon afterwards Cronje was introduced to the Indian businessman Sanjeev Chowla, and it was the mobile phone conversations with him in India that were recorded by the police. Unaware that the phone, which belonged to Chowla, was tapped, Cronje was encouraging various members of his team to under-perform. After coming clean he was banned for life, and his teammates Henry Williams and Herschelle Gibbs for six months.

In an almost incredibly cruel twist of fate, Cronje himself was later killed in a plane crash on a domestic flight in South Africa. His legacy, far from what might have been imagined by a dispassionate spectator at Lord's on that sunlit June day in 1998, is a dark one. What lurks behind the apparently innocent scenery of a cricket match? How significant is it that a batsman was out for less than 20, or that the first over wasn't a maiden? Post-Cronje and perhaps for as long as the game is played, we may well wonder.

the root of whose problem, as he later admitted, was "an unfortunate love of money". He took it, although he later claimed he lied to Gupta about match-fixing. And having become addicted Cronje could not stop. In 2000 he accepted 53,000 rand and a leather jacket for his wife from the bookmaker Marlon Aronstam, in return for "making

OPPOSITE Mohammad Azharuddin batting for India in 1999

BELOW The England team celebrate victory over South Africa in the Cronje-contrived fifth Test at Centurion Park, 2000

Nets

NETS FEATURE PROMINENTLY in cricket terminology. Net run rate is increasingly used as a means of dividing teams who finish level on points in a tournament. Net profit, or loss, is a crucial component of the balance sheet when clubs publish their accounts at the end of the year. Neither, however, is anticipated in quite the same way as the nets in which the players hone their skills during practice.

Throughout the modern history of the game, nets have been used for this purpose. As facilities have become more sophisticated, so the variety of nets has increased so that there is a type of net to suit nearly every situation. There are nets with artificial wickets, nets that can be rolled out to use on the edge of the square and nets indoors. When good, all of them provide an excellent place in which coaches can work with players to help them make advances in their game. If they fall below the required standard, they can be a positive danger, both physically and to confidence.

Cricket can be a dangerous game at the best of times, with a hard ball being propelled or hit at speed. On poor surfaces, this can become highly dangerous, but this is only one respect in which nets can pose a serious threat to safety. The

old days when little attention was paid to the quality of turf net pitches have hopefully gone for good. Many a promising young player was lost to the game with confidence shattered by balls, often delivered at pace from considerably less than 22 yards, that would leap alarmingly from a length or creep along the ground. Neither batsman nor bowler learns anything useful in such conditions.

Even artificial pitches need some sort of maintenance, while they also need to be of sufficient dimensions. In order to keep down the costs of construction, there are examples of artificial net pitches that come to an end barely beyond the length of a short ball. There is nothing worse for a batsman facing a quick bowler who drops the ball short and finds the edge of the pitch construction. From there it can fly in a totally unpredictable fashion.

That is not the extent of the dangers inherent in nets. Especially when sited indoors, the lighting can be totally inadequate for cricket, as can the background. There might be holes in the dividing net between bays, or the anchoring at the foot of dividing nets can be loose, allowing the ball to pass underneath. Frequently these dividing nets do not extend far enough, so failing to protect bowlers and others at the non-striker's end from balls driven back by the batsman.

It is not always the bowlers that need protection in such circumstances. The story goes that in his early days with Derbyshire, Devon Malcolm was distinctly quick, but somewhat erratic. The county captain at the time was Kim Barnett who was not a little disconcerted

OPPOSITE The days of CB Fry and poor quality outdoor nets have long gone

BELOW England players train in the indoor nets at Lord's

by a particularly rapid ball from Malcolm that, in poor light, whistled past his nose without bouncing. Barnett just managed to get out of the way as the thunderbolt from Malcolm crashed into the back netting. He was not wearing a helmet, but then why should he have been? He was in the spinners' net alongside the one in which the wayward Malcolm was operating!

When the indoor nets at Derbyshire were first built, they were considered to be a great advance in facilities. This was despite the fact that they consisted of nothing more than a roll of green linoleum laid on a concrete base, all within an elongated Nissen hut. At the official opening of the new facility, Donald Carr took advantage of his position as captain to take the first knock.

He was delighted by the way the ball came nicely onto the bat off the lino, and was enjoying himself going through an array of strokes. It was at this point that one of the great seamers of his time, Les Jackson, arrived to bowl. Having creamed all the others around, Carr faced Jackson's first ball that jagged back off the seam and struck him a painful blow on the inside of his thigh. He played three balls from other bowlers before Jackson loped in again to bowl with his slingy action and got another ball to jag back to strike him in the same place.

As he rubbed furiously at his smarting inner thigh, Carr decided that he had been batting for long enough and it was time to let someone else have a go. He spoke to Jackson as he passed, asking how it was, when everyone else was unable to get any deviation, he was getting it to dart all over the place. "Because it's a green wicket, skip," was Jackson's laconic reply.

Bowling on a concrete base is not ideal, especially for pace bowlers. There is no 'give' in concrete or similar unforgiving landing areas at the bowler's end. It has been suggested that the increased incidence of back and leg injuries in young quick bowlers is the result of too much bowling on such surfaces. Similar dangers occur when turf footholds are badly worn and uneven.

For all the dangers, however, well-managed and properly maintained nets can be a huge help to players and coaches alike. They give the opportunity to experiment, to work on various aspects of play and to prepare a player for the real thing to come out in the middle. That is, providing he is the type of player who enjoys playing in nets. Some simply do not enjoy the confines of the cage.

On the tour of India in 1984/85, England's Graeme Fowler was in such poor form in the nets before the Madras Test that he swung at his discarded helmet with his foot, planting it in the side of the net as if he was a footballer from Old Trafford rather than a cricketer, before going for some throw-downs on a patch of outfield. Fortunately, he left his frustrations and form in the net and proceeded to record his highest Test innings of 201 in the match that started next day.

Ian Botham was another who did not really take to net practice. Even as a youngster on the Lord's ground staff, he liked to go for all his shots rather than concentrating on any defensive skills. After yet another great swing of the bat, the coach, Len Muncer, admonished Botham by saying: "No, no, no. Just look at where your feet are." The young Botham's riposte was: "Never mind my feet; look where the ball is," motioning in the general direction of Baker Street.

ABOVE Graeme Fowler of England celebrates his double century during the fourth Test against India in Madras, 1985

OPPOSITE England's Andrew Flintoff in the nets at The Wanderers, Johannesburg, January 2005

Out

THE MOMENT, HABIT-ually the most dramatic in cricket, arouses utterly contrasting emotions. For the batsman, it can be one of annihilating finality. Geoff Boycott used to say that whenever it hap-pened to him he felt sick inside, although history indicates that not all his team mates, accomplished batsman though he was, invariably shared the same sensation.

For the bowler it is one of varying degrees of triumph, depending mainly on the state of the game at the time, the class of the batsman and the quality of the delivery that achieved the dismissal. For any fielder involved it is broadly similar, although the standard of the catch, stumping or run out may likewise affect the extent of the celebration.

There remain ten ways in which a batsman can be dismissed, and although this is an age-old cricket question, many would still be hard put to it to reel them off in a trice. They are: bowled, timed out, caught, handled the ball, hit the ball twice, hit wicket, leg before wicket, obstructing the field, run out and stumped. Half of these might reasonably be termed regular modes of dismissal, the others are rather rarer.

In terms of sheer drama, the end of Don Bradman's Test career at The Oval in 1948 must take some beating. The ground was packed (to twice its capacity if you believe everyone who told you that they were there). The batsman, the greatest in the history of the game, was playing what proved to be his final innings and needed just four runs to take his average past the hundred mark. Perhaps struggling with the emotion of the occasion following his welcome to the wicket, he was bowled, second ball, by Eric Hollies for a duck.

Nearly thirty years later, the first World Cup final started with a bang at Lord's when the diminutive Guyanese left-hander Roy Fredericks hooked the great Dennis Lillee, then in his prime, and the ball headed for St. John's Wood Road. Barely anyone watching had noticed that Fredericks, slipping while he played the stroke, had dislodged both bails. As the ball cleared the boundary by several yards, he was being given out hit wicket.

At Edgbaston in 1999, a game that ranks arguably as the finest one-day international ever played ended in unimaginable drama. Australia were playing South Africa in the semi-final of the World Cup and Lance Klusener, their bludgeoning left-hander, had taken 31 runs off 14 balls to leave South Africa just one run short of victory with one wicket in hand and four balls to be bowled. The first was hit straight by Klusener and Allan Donald, the non-striker, was almost run out as he backed up too far. Instead of heeding the warning, Klusener repeated the shot next ball and charged. Donald had to guard against a deflection running him out

OPPOSITE Dennis Lillee traps Geoff Boycott LBW to become the record Test wicket taker

BELOW The fateful moment - Don Bradman bowled Eric Hollies 0, The Oval 1948

ABOVE Not a pretty sight for Allan Donald as he is run out in the famous 1999 World Cup semi-final to hand a place in the final to Australia

and so grounded his bat, but dropped it and set off woefully late to be run out by yards. The match was tied, but Australia went through on net run rate to dispatch Pakistan in the final.

Two years later Michael Vaughan became only the seventh batsman in Test history to be dismissed handled the ball. Vaughan was in prime form during the third Test against India at Bangalore in 2001. He had already stroked eight

fours when he went down on one knee to sweep Sarandeep Singh for another. The ball struck his pad, went up in the air through a tangle of gloves, bat and arms, came down onto his thigh and, as it landed in front of him, the batsman trapped it with his glove before tossing it away.

It was not going to roll back onto the stumps. It was not going to be caught. Nevertheless, the bowler was quite entitled to appeal under Law 33.1 and Vaughan had to go. He is in good company. The only other Englishman to suffer the same fate was Graham Gooch, while the previous man out in this manner was Steve Waugh in Chennai in 2001. By one of those strange quirks, the umpire who upheld the appeal against Waugh was none other than AV Jayaprakash, who quite rightly sent Vaughan on his way for the same offence. South Africa's Russell Endean, Andrew Hilditch of Australia, Pakistan's Mohsin Khan and the Barbadian Desmond Haynes complete the melancholy list.

The great England batsman Len Hutton has a unique distinction. He is the one player to be dismissed obstructing the field in Tests. After top edging a ball in the fifth Test against South Africa at The Oval in 1951, he played at it a second time to defend it from hitting the stumps, but in the process prevented the wicketkeeper Endean – who seems to feature in these strange dismissals - from taking a catch. There is no record of a batsman being timed out or dismissed hit the ball twice in Tests.

Run outs are always an infuriating death for the batsman, but never more so than when he is the victim of a deflection when backing up. Warwickshire's John Jameson, a sturdy opener who played in four Tests, had more than his share of run outs, being the victim of three in his first four innings for England. At The Oval in 1971 he had already suffered the fate once, after making his best score of 82, when in the second innings the India spinner Bhagwat

BELOW Michael Vaughan looks on in disbelief as the Indian team celebrate his dismissal for handling the ball in Bangalore, 2001

Chandrasekhar deflected a straight drive from Brian Luckhurst into the stumps, with Jameson out of his ground. It was the only instance of an Englishman being run out twice in the same Test. Chandrasekhar proceeded to run through the England side, and India won their first-ever Test series in England.

When a batsman is actually given out by the umpire, there is a dreadful finality about it. The man in the white coat needs a hard streak in his soul to end the batsman's participation in the game.

OPPOSITE Umpire Javed Akhtar raises the dreaded finger

BELOW Sameer Dighe of India appeals and Steve Waugh is given out after handling the ball during the third Test, Chennai, 2001

Some find it harder than others. There is a story from a country house game where the titled landowner ordered his butler to stand as umpire. The awful moment inevitably arrived when the butler had to answer an appeal from square leg as to whether his employer had made his ground for a run. Being unable to utter the words "that's out", the butler merely raised his finger and said: "I am afraid His Grace is not in."

Pavilion

IRREFUTABLY, THEY COME IN ALL shapes and sizes. Without exception, their interiors have been the backcloth for agony and ecstasy and everything between, individual and collective. Here, coach and captain will issue their briefings before play, or exhortations to do better after lunch or tea. Here, inquests will be held after defeat, or champagne corks may pop in celebration of victory.

Here, too, bats might be flung down in fury by batsmen who believe that they have been unfairly triggered by an incompetent umpire. And it can be a lot worse than that. More than one fortuitously situated plate of glass in a door or a window has been shattered over the years, as returning players have given still fuller vent to their disgust.

When a batsman has been controversially dismissed, the dressing room can

ABOVE The original pavilion at The Oval

be an inner sanctum. It is wise to leave him there on his own for a little while, to vent his spleen and re-emerge in his own time. Conversely, if he has returned in triumph after completing a century, the same room will, in a trice, be in a ferment of back-slapping and celebration. The spirit of cricket embraces a certain degree of decorum on the field; in the pavilion there is the chance to unwind, to let off steam.

Other functions vary enormously. On a first visit to a ground, word may get

PAVILION

around that the showers are indifferent, or worse. Suspiciously, pessimistically, the first player bold enough to experiment will take tentative steps to establish the truth. By the time he gets to grapple gingerly with the tap and heat adjuster, he may already have discovered that the use of the plural was an exaggeration, that there is only one shower for eleven people, and that it is cold, or lukewarm, or produces little more than a dribble. Then again, it might only be when he is covered from head to toe in

soap and shampoo that the heat adjuster does not work and by the time he wants to rinse off the lather that the water is, by now, some way beyond boiling point.

And then of course there is the food, upon which so much of a club's reputation may depend. What will appear for tea? Will there be smoked salmon in the sandwiches, or boring old fishpaste? Is the bread fresh? Will there be scones, strawberry jam and clotted cream, and if so, what are the chances of getting back

RIGHT The elegant pavilion at Liverpool Cricket Club, Aigburth

on to the field? And what next? With a following wind, a sumptuous chocolate cake, made that day by the home captain's mother. And crucially, will the tea itself be of the right strength?

As the grade of pavilion rises, so the facilities improve. A bar perhaps, with – glory be – draught beer, or at least some bottles and cans to open and unwind with at close of play. Possibly even an integrated score box and board, enabling the inevitable scoring shift to be worked in some degree of comfort. And then the trimmings, serried ranks of framed photographs of bygone elevens, badges and mottos, honours boards, a flagstaff, perhaps even two. And maybe there will even be the luxury of a television, for monitoring England's progress in the Test.

Of course, if you get to play in a Test, or even at first-class level, you can expect all this and more. Pavilions at county grounds are far more substantial, and include large public areas where members can take their ease. Aesthetically they vary, and at some grounds the areas reserved for the players are no longer in a pavilion at all, as at Headingley where they are hidden within the huge complex of the football

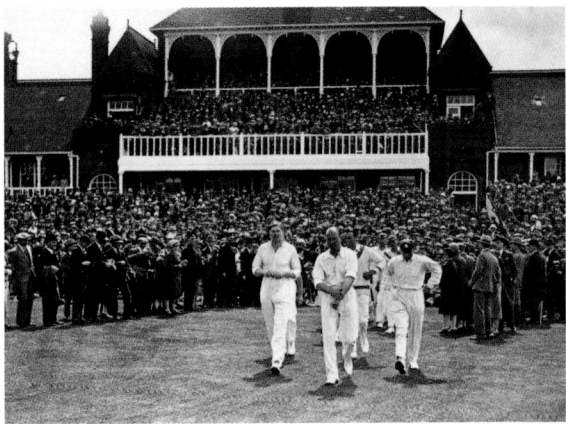

stand. The former pavilion there, a prosaic brick-built affair, is now used as the Yorkshire County Cricket Club offices.

For more than a century the last word in pavilions, in England and probably the world, has adorned Lord's Cricket Ground in its Victorian splendour. Designed in 1889 by the architect FT Verity, who also had a hand in the design of the Royal Albert Hall 18 years earlier, it is the third to be built at cricket's headquarters. The first burned down in 1825, and its replacement was dismantled to make room for the present building, rebuilt on a Sussex estate and eventually demolished to make

ABOVE The old pavilion at Headingley looms large behind Arthur Carr's England side as they take the field during the third Test against Australia, 1926

way for property development nearly a century later.

No such upheaval could possibly be envisaged for the existing structure, which was built to symbolise the Marylebone Cricket Club's then pre-eminent status in the game. It has only once been closed, in the winter of 2004/5 for a multi-million pound refurbishment. It boasts two large towers at either end, each sporting the MCC monogram and flagpoles, up which are run the representative dusters of the two participating teams. There is a changing room in each tower, from which progress to the middle of the pitch is a comparatively lengthy process.

After descending almost to ground level, the incoming batsman passes through cricket's hallowed hall, the Long Room, where he will cross with his outgoing team mate before going out through the door, down a gentle stone stairway between the benches populated by MCC members, before he finally sets foot on the sacred turf. Provided, that is, he has not taken a wrong turning, as Northamptonshire's David Steele did as he was going out to play his maiden Test innings, inadvertently going down an extra staircase and emerging, not in the open air, but in the club conveniences. In a building not associated with the lighter side of cricket, he would have encountered a delightfully whimsical piece of humour. The doors are not labelled 'In' and 'Out', but 'Out' and 'Not Out'.

Since the pavilion was built, the MCC's administrative powers have diminished, passing in the main to the body now known as the England and Wales Cricket Board, whose offices are at the other end of the ground. But the MCC continues to be the guardian of the Laws of Cricket, and its officers still meet in the Committee Room in the pavilion. The Long Room itself is festooned with magnificent pictures and other cricket memorabilia. The building may no longer be the game's power base, but its serene opulence still carries a certain aura, reflecting the game's time-honoured traditions like nowhere else on earth.

ABOVE Nasser Hussain in the Long Room at Lord's after announcing his retirement from cricket on May 27, 2004

OPPOSITE David Steele taking on the Australians at Lord's in1975, having eventually found his way from the dressing room to the middle

Quicks

WHEN STEPHEN HARMISON tore through the West Indies batting on the fourth morning of the first Test at Sabina Park in March 2004, his performance added an extra frisson of excitement for England supporters. Quite apart from turning what had been an even contest into a rout, it confirmed the promise that Harmison had shown at home and abroad over the previous few months. That much sought-after rarity in English cricket, an out-and-out quick, had been unearthed once more.

Harmison contributed more than anyone to England's eventual 3-0 series win, although he received excellent support from England's three other pacemen, Andrew Flintoff, Matthew Hoggard and Simon Jones. By the end of the following summer, when England had won all seven of their Tests at home, Harmison was rated the world's number one bowler.

In terms of wickets Bob Willis stands tallest for England, even above Fred Trueman, who was the first of all bowlers to the 300 mark. Between the two came John Snow, a fine athlete with a rhythmic action who tended to save his

ABOVE RIGHT
Stephen Harmison celebrates taking the wicket of Shivnarine Chanderpaul during the first Test between West Indies and England at Sabina Park, March 2004

QUICKS

78 | THE LITTLE BOOK OF CRICKET

best for Tests, particularly against Australia. Willis, all glazed eyes and arm-pumping aggression, suffered from not having a regular bowling partner (the role was often filled by Ian Botham), while Trueman undoubtedly benefited from the steadiness of Brian Statham at the other end. And before Trueman came Alec Bedser, that formidable purveyor of medium-fast inswing.

After Willis's retirement, England's two most successful quicks were Darren Gough and Andrew Caddick. When both fit they complemented each other well. Gough, of limited height but huge

heart, was loved by crowds and dubbed England's talisman for the lift he gave to the team. Caddick, whose height allowed him that critical extra bounce, was frequently written off as an awkward character early in his career, but found in Nasser Hussain a captain to make him tick. Angus Fraser's success in the Caribbean in 1998 was perhaps the crowning achievement of an excellent career, while no one who saw Devon Malcolm's explosive demolition of South Africa at The Oval in 1994 will forget it.

Delving further back into history, the names of Harold Larwood and Bill Voce will forever be associated with the

ABOVE Hansie Cronje's middle stump is uprooted by Devon Malcolm on his way to those incredible figures of 9 for 57 at The Oval, 1994

OPPOSITE Fred Trueman takes his 300th Test wicket as Neil Hawke of Australia is caught by Colin Cowdrey, August 1964

ABOVE A portrait of Australian fast bowler Frederick 'The Demon' Spofforth from 1880

OPPOSITE The unmistakable action of Jeff Thomson from the 1983 Ashes series in Brisbane

Bodyline series of 1932/33. According to contemporaries Larwood was as fast then as they come, but he did not play for England again afterwards. Another meteor flashed briefly across the skies 22 years later, as Frank Tyson ripped through Australia's batting in 1954/55, and South Africa's in England the following season. Before any of these Sydney Barnes, though not of top pace, was a performer of critical importance for England in the early 20th century, and Maurice Tate, who turned from slow to quick, took 155 wickets in just 39 Tests.

Perhaps the earliest quick to become a household name was an Australian. "The Demon" Frederick Spofforth was a key figure in the early development of Australian cricket, and played regularly against England in the 1880s, taking 14 wickets to carry Australia to victory in the first Ashes match in 1882. His legacy is a proud one, stretching all the way down to Glenn McGrath, one of the greatest to play the game, and Brett Lee, one of the fastest. In an age when pace could be measured a good deal more accurately than in the days of Spofforth, Lee broke the 160 km/h barrier during the 2003 World Cup. Possessed of a devastating yorker, his comparative pace to Pakistan's Shoaib Akhtar was the source of much media hype.

Australians too hunt better in pairs – witness Ray Lindwall and Keith Miller after the war - and perhaps did so most devastatingly in the mid 1970s, when Dennis Lillee was joined by a man with an almost freakish action, Jeff Thomson, to terrorise batsman around the world. Lillee's approach to the wicket in his pomp was fantastic to watch in its raw, flowing splendour,

while Thomson's delivery, the ball slung from behind his shoulder, made it hard for batsmen to see it with anything like the time they needed. After their time Craig McDermott was Australia's key quick of the 1980s, while Merv Hughes was as well known for his complexion and language as for his achievements with the ball. Jason Gillespie, although injury-prone, was also to become a world-class quick.

Shoaib Akhtar, who burst on to the scene in the 1999 World Cup, was not the first Pakistan bowler to succeed with pace. Imran Khan, lithe and athletic, was perhaps the most famous, although Wasim Akram, one of a handful of bowlers to pass the 400 mark, heads their list of wicket-takers. And when it came to toe-crushers, who wanted to be "Waqared"? Waqar Younis was magnificent, and his partnership with Wasim in their earlier years could be devastating. Neighbours India, more noted for spin, have produced two fine and durable quicks in Kapil Dev, their great all-rounder, and Javagal Srinath. And although no bowler of express pace has emerged from Sri Lanka, Chaminda Vaas has served them to guileful effect at fast-medium.

In southern Africa, the man they called "White Lightning" struck more than anyone else. Allan Donald was one of the great modern quicks, and his duel with Mike Atherton at Trent Bridge in 1998 remains one of the most compelling passages of play in recent years. Two Pollocks – Peter before isolation and his nephew Shaun since – have also made huge contributions. Neighbours Zimbabwe's impact on Test cricket would have been still more limited without the Herculean effort of their prime bowler, Heath Streak. Returning to the Antipodes, no quick in the world

ABOVE Waqar Younis celebrates taking the wicket of Marcus Trescothick first ball during the England v Pakistan One-Day International at Headingley 2001

QUICKS

has been more accomplished or consistent than Richard Hadlee, who led New Zealand's attack in the 1970s and 80s.

There is surely no sight more awesome than a genuinely fast bowler in his prime, or more daunting than a pair of them operating in harness. When it comes to four in the same team, which West Indies were able to field in the 1980s, history tells us that there is little chance of withstanding the barrage.

It was an Antiguan, Andy Roberts, who set the tone, with a deceptively relaxed run up that preceded extreme pace and a lethal bouncer. Michael Holding's approach, so quiet that the umpire could hardly hear it, was known as "Whispering Death", and his display on an Oval featherbed in 1976 was immortal. At six foot seven, Joel Garner possessed the last word in yorkers, while Malcolm Marshall, swift, skiddy and resilient, was perhaps the greatest of them all. But none was more durable than Courtney Walsh, the first to pass 500 wickets, or meaner than Curtly

Ambrose, another of the game's literal and metaphorical giants.

With the retirement of Walsh, the lethal production line ended. With it went West Indies' invincibility, passing to Australia, who in McGrath, Gillespie and Lee had a formidable pace attack of their own. That mere fact illustrates how influential extreme pace can be. The West Indies' attack may have been unbalanced, even monotonous at times in the 1980s and 1990s, but it was unarguably one of the most effective in the history of the game.

OPPOSITE
The famous Curtly Ambrose celebration – Mike Atherton was on the receiving end of this LBW decision in Trinidad, 1994

BELOW
Atherton and Allan Donald exchange "pleasantries" during the fourth Test match at Trent Bridge, 1998

Runs

OF ALL CRICKET'S INTRICATE records, is any more prized than the individual one for runs scored in Test cricket? One man – Brian Lara – has the unique distinction of having broken it twice, after reaching an astonishing 400 not out against England in Antigua in April 2004. Great cricketers – Bradman, Hutton and Sobers among them – have held it, and it was Sobers whom Lara had overtaken on the same ground ten years earlier. He reclaimed the record from Matthew Hayden, who passed Lara's 375 in October 2003. Of course no record is unbreakable, but Lara's 2004 achievement almost suspends the imagination.

Nothing is more fundamental to the state of the game than the number of runs scored. Runs are the bottom line,

the means of determining the likelihood of victory or defeat, the measure of an individual batsman's form, and in one-day cricket they must be scored with a time factor constantly in mind. When

ABOVE Brian Lara celebrates his world record-breaking innings of 400* in Antigua

is of enormous value to batsmen needing to extricate their team from a tight situation. So too is the ability to turn ones into twos, and twos into threes. The pressure can rapidly shift on to the fielding side, overthrows may result, and the complexion of the match may suddenly be altered. And if the batsman is capable of it, nothing can turn a match on its head like out-and-out attack.

One of the great joys of cricket is that no match scenario is ever exactly the same. Mentally, batsmen need to adapt to different situations every time they go in. Usually, they need to tailor their individual styles to respond. But a batsman who is a genuine, individual match-winner is a priceless asset to any team. In the 1981 Ashes series England were doubly fortunate to have a player capable of winning a match with either bat or ball, and without him they could not possibly have won the series. Neither could he have won it with the ball had it not been for the runs he scored.

runs dry up, the psychological pressure on the batsman grows. When they flow freely, the fielding captain must scratch his head and consider how to stem them.

The sharp single, constantly sought and aggressively run to rotate the strike,

An out-of-form Ian Botham resigned the captaincy after a miserable start to the rubber, which left England 1-0 down with four matches to play. Wisely, the selectors turned to his old mentor Mike Brearley, who perceptively asked

LEFT The odds on the
third Ashes Test 1981
before Botham's innings

Botham whether he wanted to play in the next game at Headingley. Although the answer was an emphatic yes, the situation when he went in to bat on day four, with his team, after following on, 105 for five, still needing 123 runs to make Australia bat again, was hardly encouraging.

As has been widely chronicled his innings, after a circumspect start, became an extreme example of an aggressive response to a losing situation. Having booked out of the hotel that morning, he suggested to his partner Graham Dilley that they should give the ball a bit of a whack. Dilley provided the initial impetus, and after tea runs flowed in directions ranging freely from the orthodox to the outrageous. Australia's hitherto dominant attack of Dennis Lillee, Terry Alderman and Geoff Lawson was run ragged.

The psychological damage Botham's innings did to Australia was massive, quite apart from leaving them a tricky little victory target that they had not expected. Bob Willis finished them off the following day, and almost incredibly

ABOVE Chris Tavare on his way to a crucial 78 in the fifth Ashes Test at Old Trafford, 1981

the greatest in Test history, Botham had wrested back the initiative.

With the dour Chris Tavare at the other end Botham again started quietly, with just three singles from his first 30 balls. He was on 28 when Australia took the new ball and the fireworks started. The great Lillee was hooked for three sixes in two overs, two of them almost off Botham's eyebrows (he was batting bareheaded). And there was no shortage of sharp singles either, as he and Tavare added 149 for the sixth wicket. By the time Botham was out he had made 118 in 102 balls, with six sixes and 13 fours.

While Alan Knott replaced Botham to make a sparkling half-century, Tavare's utterly contrasting innings continued until he was next out, having made 78 in 289 balls. But it was a vital contribution, and an excellent example of the value of a supporting role. As well as tailoring their approach to a given situation, batsmen do well to bat for their partners, so enabling the partnership to flourish. England won by 103 runs at Old Trafford, retaining the Ashes and securing an unassailable 3-1 series lead.

In a situation like that, England could not afford to waste even a single, so no

they went 2-1 down in the next match at Edgbaston in similar circumstances, Botham the bowler doing the job that Willis had done at Headingley.

In the second innings at Old Trafford, Botham arrived at the crease shortly after lunch with England, on 104 for five and only 205 runs ahead, in danger of squandering their advantage. Runs had been desperately hard to come by so far that day; just 34 had been scored for the loss of four key wickets. Australia's bowlers had apparently brought them back into the match. By that evening, after an innings that was surely one of doubt they paid attention to the 18th Law of Cricket, which deals at length with the issue of short runs. Usually the issue arises when a batsman, when completing a run, unintentionally fails to ground his bat before setting off for the next one. The umpire's straightforward response in such a case is to signal "one short". However if he believes the batsman has intentionally run short his response is different. In 1975, when Kent were playing Leicestershire at Tunbridge Wells, Mike Denness ran three during a partnership with Pakistan's Asif Iqbal. However the umpires took the view that Asif had deliberately run one of them short, and docked all three as a result.

Law 18 now states that this should be done as a matter of course, and that a "first and final" warning should be given to the batsman that the practice is unfair. If it is repeated in the innings by the same or any other batsman, the umpire will 'report the occurrence, with the other umpire, to the Executive of the batting side and any governing body responsible for the match, who shall take such action as is considered appropriate against the captain and player or players concerned'. In addition, five penalty runs are awarded to the fielding side. The same now applies if the ball hits a helmet when it has been placed on the ground behind the wicket-keeper, at which point the ball is declared dead.

Such is the importance of runs, the word is included in the title of many a cricketer's autobiography. "Runs in the Family", "In Search of Runs," and "Runs Galore" are just a few examples. Slightly hackneyed they may seem, but the underlying message is simple: what on earth would cricket and cricketers do without them?

BELOW Asif Iqbal in action for Kent

Scoring

"IF YOU'RE NOT PLAYING to win, don't bother to keep the score." Why is it difficult to read that sentence without hearing an Australian accent in the mind's ear? It certainly reveals a ruthless streak. Nothing about the joys to be derived from the game; nothing about a good match; just the uncompromising assertion that sport is played to win and to finish second is no different to finishing one hundred and second – you are still a loser.

The interesting thing about that seemingly harsh opening sentiment is that it contains mention of one of the three categories of individuals whose names appear on any scorecard. There are the players, the umpires and the scorers. No coaches, no managers and often not even the twelfth man.

Commercial necessity sometimes demands that the sponsors appear on the card as well, but there is no doubt that the scorers occupy one of the three principal roles in a game of cricket.

To be fair, this is probably because it was the scorers who produced the finished record of the game. Often unpaid and otherwise unsung, it was the scorers themselves who decided that they deserved a little of the limelight that shone on the others.

The earliest full record of a cricket match appeared in 1744 after Kent had played England at the Artillery Ground, situated in Finsbury just north of the City of London. It was in the same year that the first edition of the Laws of Cricket appeared, including reference to notches rather than runs. This was because the first method of recording the score was to indeed cut notches in a piece of wood, and scorers were referred to as notchers.

It was not until the beginning of the nineteenth century that reference was made to runs rather than notches, but by 1823 this had become a commonplace expression. It was about the same time that the course of the game was recorded with a pen on paper rather than with a knife on wood, making the change in terminology understandable.

The scorers even have their own section of the Laws, with the 2000 Code, as produced by the MCC, reading:

Law 4:

1. Appointment of scorers

Two scorers shall be appointed to record all runs scored, all wickets taken and, where appropriate, the number of overs bowled.

2. Correctness of scores

The scorers shall frequently check to ensure that their records agree. They shall agree with the umpires, at least at every interval, other than a drinks interval, and at the conclusion of the match the runs scored, the wickets that have fallen and, where appropriate, the number of overs bowled.

3. Acknowledging the signals

The scorers shall accept all instructions and signals given to them by the umpires. They shall immediately acknowledge each separate signal.

It is not a vast weight of legislation to cover what is a vital job. Furthermore, the scorer's duties seldom end there. Over the years it became traditional that the scorer would be the team's accountant and general business manager. The

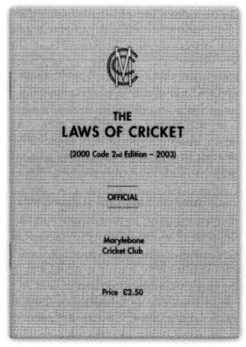

ABOVE MCC's Laws of Cricket handbook

OPPOSITE This 1947 Regency-style cricket match features a scorer notching the runs on a stick

SCORING

who made a point in the 1840s of keeping a note of his score on the stiff shirt-front that was the fashion in those days. It has to be said that at a time of heavy betting on cricket and the allied corruption that pervaded all aspects of the game, such a record was likely to prove more accurate than that of the official scorers, who might have vested interests in manipulating totals.

The modern system of scoring based on the latest technology is rather more reliable than notches on wood or pen on paper, or even a starched shirtfront. The variety of information recorded by today's scorers would be staggering to old-fashioned scribes. Not only do computers record the score, but they can produce instant analysis of the statistics and even pictorial records of where runs were scored. The idea of dots and strokes carefully recorded in a score-book appears to be a thing of the past.

Computers are also used in the way the work of the scorers is relayed to the public. The scores appear on computer screens almost instantaneously, while they are sent directly from computer to computer to enable them to be printed in newspapers without the necessity for laborious typesetting.

affinity between the two roles is obvious. And moving into the modern era, players and coaches demand rather more by way of information than simple bowling analyses or batting statistics. They want to know how and where the runs were scored.

That is where the advantages of computerisation become evident in cricket. The game has moved on from notches and paper, and even from Nicholas Wanostrocht, or Felix as he was known, the legendary batsman of All-England

On the grounds themselves, computers come into play to feed information to the scoreboard. On major grounds, the scoreboards with numbers on rollers clicking into place are rarities, while those that relied on tin plates being slotted into gaps on the fascia are even more ancient. Vast electronic displays give the spectators a wealth of information, often in an eye-catching and innovative way.

Such scoreboards are the way of the modern game, especially as they can carry advertising messages with the score or, during intervals, instead of the score. They do, however, become infuriating when a technical glitch renders them out of order or a spectator looks to catch up on a statistic during the lunch interval only to find the screen filled by an advertisement.

The art of recording the scores of a cricket match might have come a long way since the days of the notchers but, like so much else in the game, efficiency has taken over at the expense of charm. Electronic scoreboards are all very well, but the older boards were more aesthetically pleasing to the eye, especially at Trent Bridge where ample information was provided in a modern way on a traditional scoreboard. As for the laptop replacing the leather-bound tome in which the facts of the game were lovingly recorded in copper-plate handwriting, you have to ask whether this is really progress, or just another sacrifice to the great god modernity.

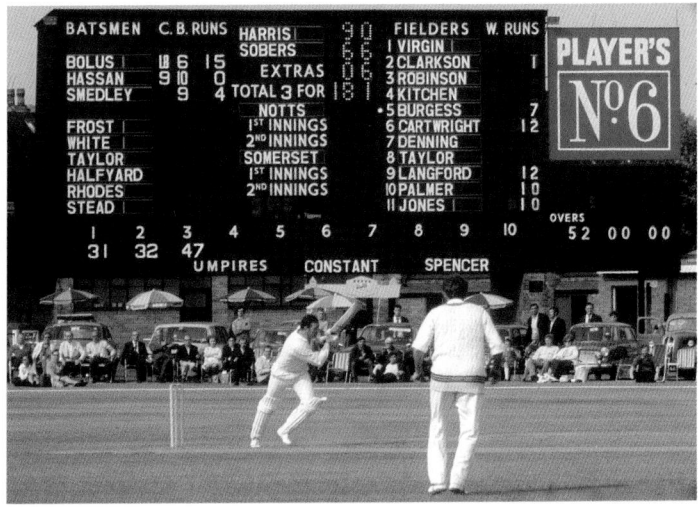

BELOW The scoreboard at Trent Bridge during a county match in the 1970s

Throwing

THROWING HAS A DEFINITE place in cricket. As a means of returning the ball from a fielder to the stumps at either end, it can be an exciting addition to the array of high-class skills on view at any match. As a means of propelling the ball from one set of stumps to the other as in bowling, it has no place whatsoever if the game is to have credibility.

Cricket is all about balances. All changes to legislation are designed to redress imbalances that occur as the game evolves. If the batsmen are gaining continued ascendancy over the bowlers, measures to restrict them are introduced. If the bowlers find some way of preventing batsmen from showing off their wares, restrictions are placed on them.

Nothing is done if there are not blatant transgressions of that natural balance. Nobody complained if there were little extra influences involved in keeping the ball in good shape. If, when cleaning the ball, the seam got ever so slightly lifted or a trace of something other than honest sweat was introduced to the polishing process, it was accepted as part of the game. As soon as ball-tampering became blatant and serious, steps were taken to eradicate it.

It is the same with throwing. If an ordinary bowler's arm does not entirely conform to the regulations concerning bending and straightening in delivery, little if any notice will be taken. If it becomes an obvious chuck, especially when either the batsman's health or the record books are under threat, something has to be done.

There is, however, a major problem with tackling this issue. To call a bowler for overstepping is to call a no ball, just as it is if a bowler is called for throwing; in both cases he has been gaining an unfair advantage and is penalised. So too is a batsman who is guilty of a short run. In all these cases, the player is being accused of cheating, whether intentionally or not, and is penalised one run. The emotive implications if a player is called for throwing are more serious.

Law 24 (3) of the MCC's Laws of Cricket states: "A ball is fairly delivered in respect of the arm if, once the bowler's arm has reached the level of the shoulder in the delivery swing, the elbow joint is not straightened partially or completely from that point until the ball has left the hand."

In the light of the publicity surrounding Muttiah Muralitharan, the outstandingly successful Sri Lankan spinner, the key phrase is

"…the elbow joint is not straightened partially or completely….". But this is where emotive considerations and undertones enter the equation.

From the moment Muralitharan shot to prominence through his extraordinary wicket-taking abilities, doubts have been expressed about the legality of his action. Some say he throws while others will go no further than saying he has a "unique, unorthodox" action. Umpires are undecided, at

OPPOSITE Ricky Ponting, one of the sharpest fielders in the game, practicing his return throw

BELOW The decidedly unorthodox bowling action of Muttiah Muralitharan

Whatever the subsequent inquiries and scientific research into Muralitharan's action, both umpires made a public statement that he had broken the rules when delivering the balls he was called for. They did not say that every ball he bowled was illegal; just the ones they called.

In the circumstances, footage showing that the bowler in question does not straighten his arm while in action is no more relevant than showing film of a bowler delivering a ball with his front foot behind the popping crease and then claiming that he should never be no balled for overstepping. All it would confirm is that he did not overstep when that particular ball was filmed, and it is the same with throwing: the filmed ball might be legal while others might not.

The Sri Lankan authorities were quick to defend their prize asset. Filming was indeed commissioned and under laboratory conditions, the University of Western Australia found that a congenital deformity prevented Muralitharan from fully straightening his right arm. Enough people seized on the evidence to proclaim his innocence and to allow him to continue with his international career. He was guilty of

least in their public pronouncements in as much as several express doubts but a very select band have come out and actually called "no ball" when Muralitharan has been bowling.

When two umpires, Ross Emerson and Darrell Hair, called Muralitharan on two separate tours of Australia, they were vilified by suggestions that there were racial undercurrents to their decision. What they had done was seen a bowler who had, in their opinion, contravened the laws of the game by throwing instead of bowling the ball. If that is what they believed, they took the correct course of action by calling the deliveries as no balls.

nothing more than being the victim of a vendetta in Australia.

Of course, the evidence proved nothing of the sort. It simply showed that he could not fully straighten his arm. It did not show that he was unable to bend his elbow at all. Look again at the wording of Law 24: "…the elbow joint is not straightened partially or completely…". Again, the relevant word is "partially".

While a spinner who throws is unlikely to threaten physical damage to a batsman, he does endanger other aspects of the game. Just imagine the ramifications if incontrovertible evidence was to emerge confirming that Muralitharan's action is illegal (or to revisit a previous position, the action employed during filming was illegal). Could his 500 wickets be struck from the record books? Would the results of matches that he played a vital role in winning be declared void? Of course not, and neither should they. The game, however, would be tarnished.

There is another legacy from allowing dubious actions to be cleared on unproven evidence. Young players watching the success of a bowler who has a questionable action can be misled into thinking that it is perfectly acceptable to copy him. Gradually, standards are eroded and the boundaries of legality are pushed further and further back until they become meaningless.

The throwing problem does not revolve around one man. There have been plenty of others who have been suspected or called. Film of the great Harold Larwood bowling during the Bodyline era suggests that his action might not have been pure. It was amazing that the Australians did not pick up on that at the time. Tony Lock, England's premier left-arm spinner in the 1950s had to remodel his action completely when he saw it on what was, at the time, sophisticated cine film.

ABOVE Harold Larwood - would his action have survived examination by slow-motion replay?

Brett Lee, Jermaine Lawson and Shoaib Akhtar are more recent high-profile international bowlers who have been forced to have remedial work done on their actions. And Muralitharan will certainly not be the last to be questioned.

Mention of Lee, Akhtar and Lawson highlight the problems when a fast bowler has a kink in his action. They are not alone among international bowlers to have come under scrutiny, but when

RIGHT Shoaib Akhtar's action has also been the subject of much scrutiny

the Australian and the Pakistani have broken the 100 mph barrier, it is not just the purity of the game and upholding of the Laws that are at stake; it could literally become a matter of life and death.

Because it is such an emotive subject, the game's governing body, the International Cricket Council, have tried to take the heat out of the situation by preventing the umpires from making instant judgements in international matches. The claim is that they can still call them in a match, but the preferred course of action is to report their suspicions to the match referee. He can then report to the player's board and the ICC Bowling Review Group who take appropriate steps.

That same body recently commissioned research into the whole question of throwing and came to the conclusion that there are a lot of bowlers that do have actions that do not conform to the Laws of Cricket. So did all those bowlers get banned? Certainly not. A degree of tolerance has been agreed to accommodate what could have been termed illegal actions.

With these processes in place, it would be a brave umpire who looks at a bowler from his position at square leg and suddenly yells "no ball". A brave umpire? Correct that to an umpire who is thinking of resigning from the international panel and who wants healthy advance sales for his forthcoming autobiography.

Umpiring

THEY ARE THE MEN WHO NEVER win the toss. While most of the players in a five-day Test match will be hoping the coin comes down in their favour so they can sit with their feet up for the best part of two days, the umpires know that they will be making their way out to the middle ready for the first ball and, five days later, will be the ones who take off the bails for the last time in the match. Apart from good eyesight and hearing, an unsurpassed knowledge of the Laws of Cricket and their interpretation and the judgement of Solomon, great physical stamina and concentration are required before anyone can contemplate donning the white coat.

The thickest of skins is no bad thing either, for the umpires' decisions usually elicit praise and scorn in equal measure. For every batsman who thinks it was slipping down the leg side, there is a bowler convinced it was knocking over all three stumps. The umpire's job is to sum up the evidence and give the decision that he believes to be right in the twinkling of an eye. Furthermore, in a Test match he will do so knowing that everyone else, with the benefit of 20:20 hindsight and a multitude of cameras trained on the action from every angle, will be instantly aware of any mistakes. One of the great surprises of cricket is that, more often than not, all the modern technology proves that the umpire was right.

Naturally, the odd howler makes the headlines, but the overall balance is vastly in favour of the umpire. If the

ABOVE Umpires Steve Bucknor and Darrell Hair share a joke during the second npower Test match between England and South Africa, July 2003

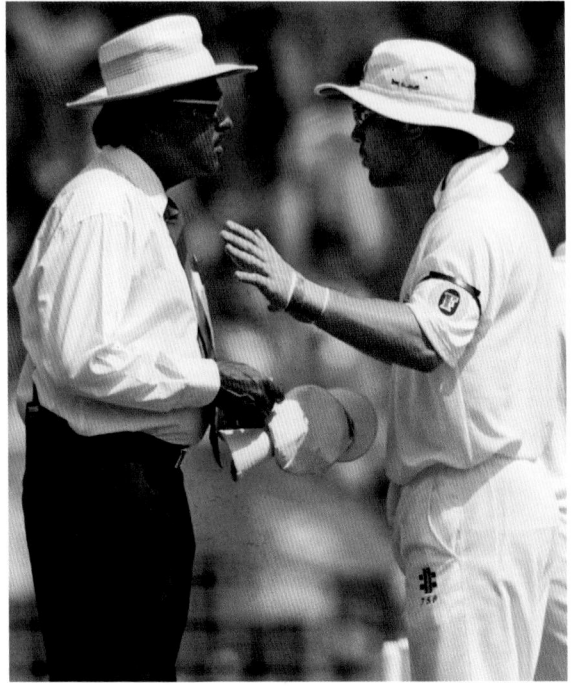

ABOVE Michael Slater remonstrates with umpire Venkat after the third umpire disallowed a catch he claimed off Rahul Dravid of India

wickets that they know are not out. It would be interesting to know if they consider themselves to be incompetent or cheats.

At the lower levels of the game, the umpire can never be proved wrong. Others might have different opinions, but the Laws of Cricket will back him up in that the outcome of any appeal depends on the umpire's opinion. Once we start considering what happens in the international arena, a new dimension is introduced, that of technology.

Whether umpires like it or not, they have to accept that, in some instances, their opinion is no longer final. There is a third umpire to which some decisions can be referred in order to consider the evidence provided by slow motion television replays. The result is that umpires on the field rarely trust their judgement in the case of run outs or stumpings. As soon as an appeal is voiced, they describe a square with their forefingers towards the third umpire's eyrie to seek the help of technology.

It has become one of the most theatrical moments in a cricket match. Players huddle together, the batsman looks at the lights that will decide his fate, while the crowd anticipates the

players who complain made as few mistakes as the umpires, they would be rewriting the record books. Players are meant only to appeal if they think the batsman is out but, if that is the case, there are some very poor judges playing the game, or they are trying to claim moment of judgement as the audience might have awaited the thumbs up or thumbs down in the Coliseum. The same type of sentiments are expressed when the red or green light appears to signify that the batsman must trudge towards the pavilion or stay to fight on.

There are those who dislike third umpire interventions, yet the argument in favour is overwhelming. Why should the umpires in the middle be forced to give an instantaneous decision that might be seen to be wrong by the rest of the world on television? Would those same critics of the system be happy to leave the outcome of a substantial wager in a horse race to the judges on the line, or would they prefer to see the evidence of the photo finish? By using replays, justice is seen to be done, and if the technology cannot determine whether a batsman is in or out, he receives the benefit of the doubt, from the umpire who is still the final arbiter.

LEFT The Australian team and the West Indian batsmen await the decision of the third umpire

ABOVE David Shepherd calls upon the services of the third umpire

OPPOSITE The most famous of them all? Umpire Dickie Bird gives Jack Russell out LBW – his last decision in Test cricket

Hawkeye does not employ the same technology as used to track missiles by the military, as was first reported. It was, however, developed from the same sort of system which, by tracking the path of the ball from different angles, can predict its future destination with a high degree of accuracy. It is whether that accuracy is acceptable or not that leads to debate.

If it were to be accepted, the system could be refined to offer umpires a graphical representation of the ball, showing where it had pitched, where it made contact with the pad and whether it would have gone on to hit the stumps. This could be relayed to a hand-held receiver, so the man in the middle could have all the relevant information in a matter of seconds.

In general, umpires do not like the idea because they fear it would render them as no more than movable hat stands who count the six balls of an over. They also claim that the technology has not been proven and that there is a possibility of error. That as opposed to the human umpire who, when it comes to lbw, has a proven record – of fallibility.

Once Pandora's box of technological tricks is opened, however, it is difficult to put the lid back on. If television replays can determine line decisions, why not call them into play to adjudicate on whether a fielder's foot touches the boundary while he has the ball, whether a catch has carried, or even whether the batsman hit it in the first place? And, with the advent of the Hawkeye system, what about lbw?

When cricket was first played, there were no umpires as such. If there were disputes, venerated former players were called upon to arbitrate. It is worth noting that even today, the players have to ask the umpires to intervene in response to an appeal rather than the match being run, for example, as by a referee in football.

As betting on cricket became prevalent, umpires became vital to ensure that the gamblers' interests were protected. They were being used by 1727 and were mentioned in the first Code of Laws in 1744. In those days, they carried bats or sticks, possibly as symbols of authority or even as a means of protecting themselves should the stakes have had a detrimental effect on the spirit of the game.

It is a feature of cricket that however much the players might disagree with a decision, any dissent is likely to be confined to a disbelieving stare or a shake of the head. Mercifully, the game has been spared the unedifying sight of officials being harangued and abused as is so common in football, baseball and other sports. If the cricket umpire no longer needs a bat or stick for self-protection, perhaps he could instead carry that monitor to help him get those tricky decisions right every time.

Village Cricket

'THE CRICKET FIELD itself was a mass of daisies and buttercups and dandelions, tall grasses and purple vetches and thistle-down, and great clumps of dark-red sorrel, except, of course, for the oblong patch in the centre – mown, rolled, watered – a smooth, shining emerald of grass, the Pride of Fordenden, the Wicket.'

Shortly after writing "England, Their England" more than 70 years ago, Archie Macdonell "awoke and found himself famous". While we will never know precisely how pivotal a part chapter seven played in this transformation, Macdonell's imaginary account of a cricket match between a Kent village and Mr. Hodge's visiting team from London remains a legendary piece of cricket literature.

It reflects its time, when England had recovered a measure of equilibrium after the Great War, and a mere six years before the country was plunged into another. For Macdonell himself, who became an author after being invalided out of the army, the idyllic picture he painted may have presented a felicitous contrast to some of his own experiences.

'Blue and green dragonflies played at hide-and-seek among the thistle-down and a pair of swans flew overhead. An

ancient man leaned upon a scythe, his sharpening-stone sticking out of a pocket in his velveteen waistcoat. A magpie flapped lazily across the meadows. The parson shook hands with the squire. The haze flickered. The world stood still.'

There have been subtle changes in the intervening years, but the broad purpose of village cricket remains the same: to be fun. This crucial trait is admirably – at times hilariously - conveyed in Macdonell's ensuing description of the match. While there is no doubting the supreme status of Test cricket then as now, consider that his book was published less than a year after the Bodyline tour of 1932/33, when the game in its upper echelons was far from fun.

Macdonell was not the first to immortalise village cricket in literature. Charles Dickens' account of the game between Dingley Dell and All Muggleton in "The Pickwick Papers" is briefer but no less empathic. Mr. Pickwick himself points out that to play such cricket, you do not necessarily need to be any good. 'I, sir, am delighted to view any sports which may be safely indulged in, and in which the impotent effects of unskilful people do not endanger human life.'

Dickens sets the village scene: 'A few boys were making their way to the cricket-field; and two or three shopkeepers who were standing at their doors, looked as if they should like to be making their way to the same spot, as

OPPOSITE Cricket being played in the 1930s in the Sussex hamlet of Ebernoe

BELOW Idyllic rural scenery surrounds a village game at Brook in Surrey

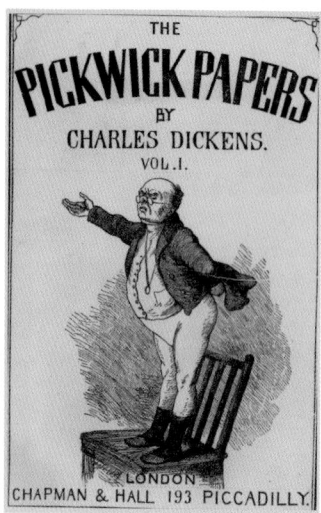

indeed to all appearance they might have done, without losing any great amount of custom thereby.' But unlike the splendid tie that concluded the Fordenden match: 'Dingley Dell gave in, and allowed the superior prowess of All Muggleton.'

Village cricket conjures much in the imagination. A patch of land, perhaps of modest size, in sight of a parish church, with a pub at hand, barrels charged for close of play. A duck pond, or river, into which a discerning, well-upholstered batsman can deposit the ball on the full. A rudimentary black scoreboard, decked by numbers on dented metal, less than pristine white paint on black. And even a copper beech inside the boundary; local rules apply if you hit it.

A smattering of easy chairs beyond the boundary edge for elderly, moustachioed spectators, the smoke from their pipes drifting lazily into the ether.

Perhaps even the odd parasol in proper sunshine, and a picnic table here and there for those who are making a day of it. Maybe a rug or two as well, adorned by the delightfully curvaceous figures of the team members' girlfriends. Enthusiastic wives (why so?), prepared to beaver away in rudimentary kitchens at the back of rickety pavilions to produce teas of varying standard, but almost invariably including cucumber sandwiches and cupcakes.

Above all, the sounds that are inseparable from the scenery. The quicker bowler's grunt of self-exertion, the consummate meeting of leather with willow, the whirr as the ball is propelled towards the boundary, the call for a run (and possibly the ensuing comedy), the thudding feet of the intervening fielder, and the appeals, their tones born of enquiry, bravado, or downright delight.

Has much changed since Dickens's time? In many respects undoubtedly so, depending by degree on how individual grounds are situated, and how villages have developed or declined. Certainly the present laws on drinking and driving have curtailed the after-match alcohol intake in places where home is more than walking distance away. The age of feminism has reduced the number of wives prepared to give up their Saturday afternoons to make tea, the quality of which may have declined (or conceivably improved) in consequence. Many attractive grounds have simply ceased to exist, built upon to cater for a growing population.

There has also been much develop- ment since Hambledon in Hampshire, the most famous cricket village of them all, was in its prime during the 18th cen- tury. Leagues have been formed, as has the national village knockout cup, the final of which is played at Lord's every September. The Cornish village of Troon, which memorably won it twice in a row in 1972 and 1973, and again in

BELOW Refreshment close at hand for a cluster of spectators during a game at Tilford in Surrey

1976, shares the record of three wins with St. Fagans in Glamorgan, winners in 1981, 1982 and 1991. Linton Park, Marchwiel, Goatacre, Elvaston, Caldy and Shipton-under-Wychwood have each raised the trophy twice.

Cricket itself has changed enormously, and continues to evolve at a frenetic rate at first-class level. Villages too have altered, along with the communities living in them. But it is still perfectly possible to find village cricket played in much the same manner as described above.

A favourite cricketing tale concerns the ball, hit so hard and high that virtually every fielder fancied his chances of catching it. "Thompson's catch, leave it for Thompson!" exclaimed the captain. The converging fielders spread once more, and the ball fell harmlessly to earth. Thompson was away on holiday. If that didn't happen in a village, it jolly well should have done.

RIGHT The imposing Hambledon memorial stone overlooks the famous ground in the 1970s

Wicket-keepers

NOTHING HELPS THE BALANCE OF a cricket team more than the presence of a player who has mastered more than one discipline. The term "all-rounder" is habitually applied to someone who can bat and bowl, but over the years there have been other key performers worthy of the description, particularly the wicket-keeper who, in addition to being busier in the field than anyone else, has more chance of helping to dismiss a batsman than any of his team mates. His batting, once considered merely useful, is now essential if he is to command a regular Test place.

Consider the current keepers in world cricket. Almost all of them are good enough batsmen to come in at number seven, while Adam Gilchrist and Kumar Sangakkara might well get into their national teams even if they couldn't keep wicket. Of recent, retired incumbents, Andy Flower regularly went in higher for Zimbabwe, while Alec Stewart began his record-breaking Test career as an opening batsman, and occupied every position between one

and seven. He often won the vote ahead of his great rival, Gloucestershire's Jack Russell, because of his superior batting, even though Russell, a wonderfully agile keeper, was a good enough batsman to score two Test centuries.

The debate about whether it is better to play a wicket-keeper/batsman, a batsman/wicket-keeper, or the best "pure" wicket-keeper, regardless of his batting, is one that has raged down the years. In 1976 there was an outcry amongst the wicket-keeping fraternity when Roger Tolchard was chosen as Alan Knott's deputy for the tour of India rather than Bob Taylor, then widely regarded as the best gloveman in England. In the event Tolchard played his four Tests on that tour, solely as a batsman, while Taylor

eventually flourished at international level after Knott joined Kerry Packer in 1977. There was a similar occurrence 20 years earlier, when Brian Taylor of Essex deputised for Godfrey Evans ahead of the inestimable Keith Andrew, but did not play in the Tests.

Perhaps more than any other country, England has been fortunate in producing successive wicket-keepers who could bat, or vice-versa. Stewart was probably more in the latter mould, like Les Ames, who along with Evans and Knott formed Kent's great wicket-keeping triumvirate of the 20th century. Opinions on who was best of those three inevitably vary according to the generations. Evans commanded massive support among his contemporaries, while Knott, a brilliant wicket-keeper and impishly aggressive batsman in a crisis (of which he had to confront plenty), was without peer in his time or since.

The primary role of the wicket-keeper has evolved along with cricket itself. As a general rule Knott preferred standing back to medium pace, believing that catches missed would outnumber stumpings taken standing up. The policy contrasted with some of his predecessors. Evans, for example, was renowned

for standing up to Alec Bedser, and for executing several stumping chances as a result. In fact, the overall proportion of stumpings taken by Evans is much higher – 46 out of 219 dismissals, while Knott took 19 out of 269. This also reflects a greater preponderance of faster bowling in the game today; of Stewart's 241 victims, just 14 were stumped. For Stewart and other modern keepers, the preference is for standing up to medium pace, particularly in one-day cricket, to inhibit the batsman's freedom to leave his ground.

To dive or not to dive? Another question that has exercised the minds of keepers down the years. Between the wars, when great catchers like Woolley and Hammond stood in the slips, for a keeper to dive in front of one of them might have been considered an affront, and in any event many keepers preferred to rely on rapid footwork. The modern creed is that if he instinctively feels he has a good chance of taking a catch he should go for it. One of the great action cricket photographs is of the Australian Rod Marsh, diving far to his right to poach what would have been a straightforward slip catch to Ian Chappell, dismissing Tony Greig off Gary Gilmour at Headingley in the 1975 World Cup. Politeness prevents speculation on what the Australian captain might have said to Marsh had the chance been missed.

LEFT A characteristically crisp cut from Alan Knott, England v Pakistan, Lord's 1974

BELOW The famous catch by Rodney Marsh to dismiss Tony Greig in the 1975 World Cup semi-final at Headingley

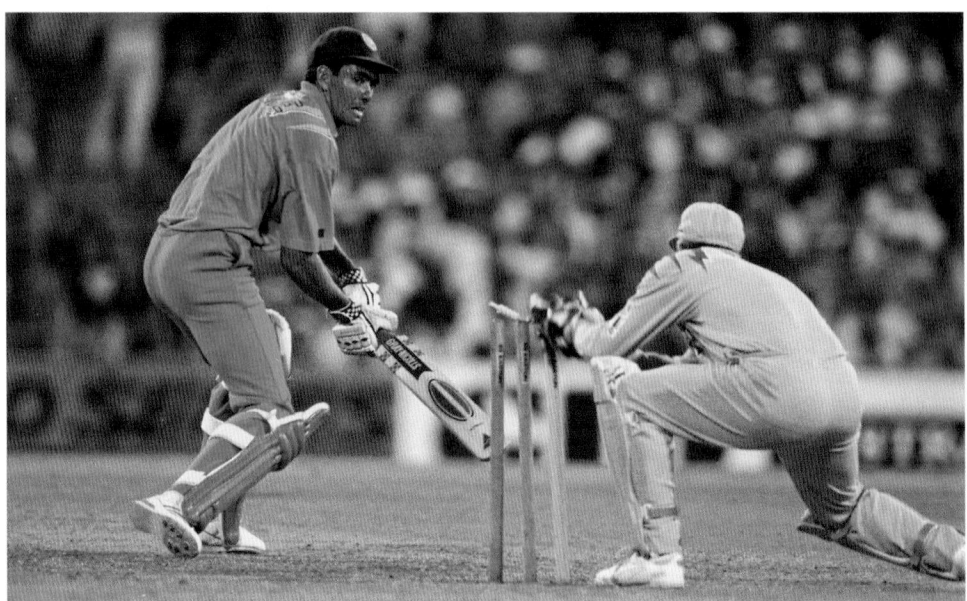

ABOVE Hansie Cronje is stumped by Ian Healy off Shane Warne in Brisbane, 1994

However spectacular such catches may be, it is broadly agreed that the most challenging part of the keeper's job is standing up to spin, especially on a turning wicket, when the batsman's body can obscure the keeper's view of the ball. The former Glamorgan and England all-rounder Peter Walker tells how the young Knott went against his advice to stand back to the off-spinner Don Shepherd, after a shower of rain had livened up the pitch at Fenners in 1964. Shepherd decided to put the impudent teenager in his place, bowling a ball that turned, lifted and sharply deflected off the inside edge. Knott caught the rising ball far to his left at shoulder height, before removing the leg bail as the batsman fell forward off balance.

Knott broke Evans's world record for

WICKET-KEEPERS

wicket-keeping dismissals in Tests, and sent champagne to Marsh when the Australian passed him in 1981. He was later overtaken by his successor, Ian Healy, who pouched an amazing 395 victims. It is a distinguished list, although like many others it reflects the greater amount of cricket played in the modern era. The South African Mark Boucher rose to third position before temporarily losing his Test place in 2004. After Boucher comes Gilchrist, followed by Jeff Dujon, the Jamaican who played when the West Indies were flattening all before them in the 1980s. Dujon was another genuine all-rounder, a joy to watch with the bat.

Other great keepers of the modern era include Wasim Bari, who missed virtually nothing for Pakistan in the 1970s, while Farokh Engineer was an asset for India. Further back, Wally Grout of Australia had a remarkable record of 187 victims from just 51 Tests. And no one can have been more appropriately nicknamed than another Australian, "The Claw", Don Tallon. Amongst the earliest to master the art was John Blackham, also of Australia, who became a legend of cricket's golden age, while Dick Lilley and Tiger Smith were famous successive England keepers of the same era.

The author of the Complete Book of Cricket, AE Knight, once wrote: "I should like to see the wicket-keeper more handsomely rewarded than he is, and I would infringe upon the delightful social communism of our fees to the extent of awarding him an extra sovereign in every match." He had a point, and who of the aforementioned distinguished band of cricketers could possibly disagree?

LEFT The man they called "The Claw": Don Tallon of Australia

X-ray

PROFESSOR WILHELM KONRAD Roentgen's name might never before have appeared in a book about cricket. However, it was in 1895 – shortly after A.E Stoddart's England side had retained the Ashes in a match that had attracted the attention of Queen Victoria - that the professor of physics at the University of Wurzberg in Bavaria discovered x-rays. It was an achievement that has had a great deal of application in a game that may well have been unknown to Professor Roentgen.

The most obvious use of x-rays in cricket is in the medical field. The combination of a hard ball and brittle bones means that players are frequent customers for the x-ray department of any hospital located close to a cricket ground. On the basis that balls are not getting any harder, either bones are becoming more brittle or there has not been a significant improvement in protective equipment, especially gloves, in recent years, as the incidence of broken fingers seems to be on the increase.

There has even been a suggestion that some players go onto the injured list because of x-rays. Not that the process causes the injuries, but because the sophistication of modern medical equipment might well show up small fractures that would previously have gone undetected. Some years ago, a batsman hit on the hand might well have gone for a precautionary x-ray that revealed nothing. Keen to retain his place in the side, the player would put his injury down to bad bruising and carry on. With even a hairline fracture showing up on a modern x-ray, the diagnosis of an injury becomes more precise and playing through pain no longer seems a sensible option.

As the technology has developed from simple x-rays to MRI scans, the diagnostic techniques available to physiotherapists have increased as well. X-rays enable bone damage to be detected, while the MRI scan can enable the study of tissue damage without surgery. Even if an operation becomes necessary, the surgeon can go straight to the damaged area and work with far greater precision. Less collateral surgical damage means a faster recovery time, and can sometimes make the difference between a player resuming his career or not.

When England fast bowler Simon Jones suffered a sickening injury in Brisbane in 2002, the first thought was that he might never be able to play at the top level again. Jones had made quite an impression, taking the first

OPPOSITE Nasser Hussain suffers a broken finger during the first Ashes Test at Edgbaston, 2001

BELOW England physiotherapist Kirk Russell attends to Simon Jones after his horrific injury at Brisbane in 2002

wicket to fall on the opening morning of the new Ashes series. It was then that he chased a ball towards the boundary and went to slide alongside it before picking it up, rising to his feet and sending in his return in the modern manner.

He chased the ball, but as he went to slide, his foot became caught in the turf, forcing all his weight into bending his knee in a direction the joint is not designed to go. The result was ruptured ligaments and nearly a year out of cricket. That could have been longer, or even worse, had not x-rays and scans revealed the exact nature of the injury and allowed the surgeons to repair the damage as efficiently as they did. It was then up to Jones to work extremely hard on getting back to fitness and, happily, returning to international cricket.

Fast bowling is one of the facets of the game where injuries are bound to occur. To sprint a distance before jumping and turning and then landing, while straining every sinew to propel the ball as quickly as possible, is to invite trouble. And trouble rarely requires a gold edged stiff card before it makes an appearance. With a modern, sedentary lifestyle increasing the fast bowler's vulnerability to injury, the problem becomes more serious despite all the work done in the field of injury prevention as well as cure.

For many years the physiologists could only work on assumptions when attempting to discover the cause of injuries. X-rays and scans could show where the damage had occurred, but they left plenty of scope for discussion as to the cause of injury. For example, general medical research revealed that an alarming proportion of young fast bowlers had suffered stress fractures in the lower back at some stage of their careers. What was causing them and how could they be prevented?

Research was conducted into surfaces, types of footwear and bowling actions that were most likely to put undue strain on the lower back. Possible preventative measures abounded, including unworkable restrictions on the number of overs that could be bowled in both matches and practice by various age groups. It is arguable that these restrictions were more damaging in the long run than the condition they were designed to overcome.

Then came the development of a system called Vicon, which allowed move-

ment specialists to see the benefits of x-rays, but while the bowler was in action. The system itself is a by-product of the film industry. It is based on a technique used for animation that can show skeletal functions while the subject is on the move.

By attaching infrared sensors to key parts on the bowler's body and relaying

ABOVE The x-ray of the Ashes urn, clearly showing the crack in the stem

biomechanists and coaches can work with the bowler to assess how his action can be made more efficient and, just as important, safer.

This might all appear to be very futuristic, but it is available now – at a considerable price. It is, therefore, reassuring to know that simple, conventional x-rays can play a part in preserving traditional aspects of the game. A dozen years before Professor Roentgen's discovery, cricket's oldest trophy came into being – the Ashes urn. The Australians were keen that the prize that was, metaphorically, in their possession for so long, should be allowed to leave the Lord's Museum to be visible to cricket enthusiasts in Australia.

The curators were opposed to the idea because they feared that the fragile little urn would be unable to withstand such a journey, however carefully it was handled. The problem was that they did not know just how fragile it was. The answer? An x-ray that revealed a crack in the stem where previous damage had been ineffectively repaired. Thanks to an x-ray, the Ashes urn, like many an injured player, has been restored to rude health.

their movement patterns through computerised equipment, it is possible to see the bowler as no more than a moving skeleton. Once this material is available,

Yips

THE BUSINESS OF BOWLING A cricket ball is not a natural movement. The best bowlers make it look as if it is, but it is not.

Just consider a process that involves running to a fixed point, jumping in the air and turning the body through 90 degrees, landing on one foot, transferring the weight to the other while lifting the arms above head-height, changing from having one shoulder pointing towards the target to having the other one pointing the same way and doing all this while rotating the arms and letting go the ball at precisely the right moment. It requires a certain measure of coordination.

Most of the time, it is achieved without a second thought. If, however, you ask a bowler to analyse his movements and think about what he is doing in the terms outlined above, the possibilities

for the coordination to go awry become alarmingly real. It is like asking someone to analyse how they breathe. While working out exactly how they manage it, the chances are that they will asphyxiate.

Cricket is a cerebral game. There are several players who have been within six

ABOVE West Indies fast bowler Malcolm Marshall making it look easy inches of being great cricketers. Unfortunately for them, the six inches in question can be measured from one ear to the other. They have the ability but not the application, especially when the time comes that the voice of doubt becomes louder than the sound of confidence coming from the depths of the mind. That is when problems occur.

It happens to the golfer with disconcerting frequency, usually on the green when he is faced with a putt of sometimes no more than a couple of feet. The golfer can sink that putt 999 times in 1000 attempts in normal circumstances. Left-handed; right-handed; one-handed; eyes open; even with eyes closed. He could sink the putt with a stick of rhubarb.

Then, on the one-thousandth occasion, from somewhere within the inner recesses of the brain comes a little whisper from Thomas – of the doubting variety. As the grains of confidence run through his fingers, the golfer starts to consider the possibility of missing, then the unlikelihood of holing, before the certainty that there is no chance of what now appears a huge ball being propelled into that tiny hole using the live eel that the putter has suddenly become. That golfer has the dreaded yips which, unfortunately, can affect bowlers as well.

This loathsome affliction need not necessarily be terminal. On the 1984/85 tour of India and Sri Lanka, England's left-arm spinner Phil Edmonds found he had trouble not with the whole process of bowling, but simply with his run-up. Despite the fact that he was not running in quickly, Edmonds found insurmountable problems in landing his front foot in the right place in the bowling stride.

His solution was to cut his run so that instead of a stately approach to the wicket by the tall bowler, he shuffled in over no more than two paces and from an almost standing position delivered the ball with such effect that he was a

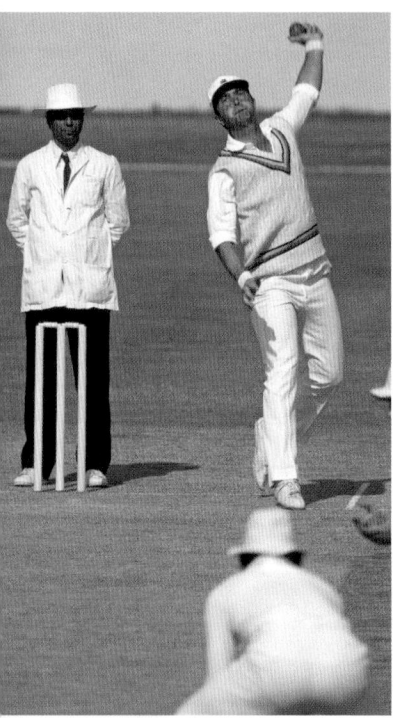

BELOW England's Phil Edmonds getting in a spin during the 1984-85 tour of India

key member of England's attack on that tour, taking 14 Test wickets.

It was not such a happy story for another member of the left-arm spinning fraternity. Keith Medlycott was a consistent performer for Surrey between 1984 and 1991. A useful lower-middle order batsman, he was a spinner of such ability that he was selected to go on England's tour to the Caribbean in 1990/91. He did not get a Test, but neither did Eddie Hemmings as the number one spinner on that tour. Nevertheless, Medlycott performed well in the first-class matches when he had the chance, including taking six wickets in the game against Barbados.

Medlycott came home to have a good season in 1991 with 49 wickets, but that was it. He did not bowl another ball for Surrey in first-class cricket as the yips took hold. At the end of 1992 he was released and, although he came back as a very successful coach at a time of Surrey dominance in domestic cricket, his playing career was sadly unfulfilled.

It is not only slow bowlers who get to the stage when they feel they cannot let go of the ball for fear of where it might go. Quicker bowlers are not

immune. Kevin Emery made a spectacular entry into first-class cricket with 83 wickets for Hampshire in his debut season. He played for England B, taking four good wickets against the Pakistanis, and was close to selection for the winter's Ashes tour.

ABOVE Keith Medlycott bowling for Surrey

At the start of the following season, he suffered a chipped bone in his ankle, tried to rush back into action and took only five wickets in his five matches. He lost so much confidence that he could not bowl again in first-class cricket at the age of 24. He tried reverting to the off-spin that had got him into the England Schools side, but it was to no avail and the yips had claimed another victim.

If such an affliction can have a lighter side, it comes in a story from Derbyshire. They had another of the blighted breed of left-arm spinners, a worthy county cricketer by the name of Fred Swarbrook. The story goes that he got a bad dose of the yips and was dropped from the first team because there was just no knowing where the ball might go. He was even dropped from the second team.

Swarbrook was so desperate to revive his career that he consulted an elderly faith healer in Ilkeston. This unlikely source of cricketing redemption gave him a pebble that he was advised to rub just before he bowled every ball. Whether it had magic powers in reality could never be established, but it worked for Swarbrook.

He got back into the second team and bowled without the trace of a problem. He was bowling well in practice, rubbing away at his pebble. Then the call came for a return to first-team cricket.

The moment arrived when he was called on to bowl. He set the field with his captain, rubbed the pebble and bowled – a ball that bounced twice and went wide. He rubbed his pebble, bowled again, only to see it sail high over the wicket-keeper's head. Another rub on the pebble, another double-bouncer. The embarrassed silence from everyone on the field was broken by a suggestion from slip. "Hey, Fred, try rubbing the ball and bowling the pebble!"

If there is anything crueller than the yips in cricket, it is the sense of humour from teammates of the afflicted.

Zoom

IT WAS ALWAYS DIFFICULT TO portray cricket to the remote viewer because of the distance between the middle, where the serious action takes place, and the boundary edge. That is why action shots of the early players tended to be staged, with the result that they appeared anything other than natural, while the athletic grace that is such a feature of cricket is missing from those early pictures. The players show all the athletic grace of wax dummies.

Then came the Great War, and with it a major advance in the means to capture photographic images from long range. Many benefits derive from military necessity, but one of the most unlikely ones was the ability to photograph cricket in close-up. The generals, some way behind the front line, appreciated the value of good reconnaissance photographs, but found that improved anti-aircraft fire meant that members of the Royal Observer Corps had to fly higher and higher if they wanted to return to base unscathed.

If those generals back at HQ were to get the photographs they wanted, longer-range camera lenses had to be

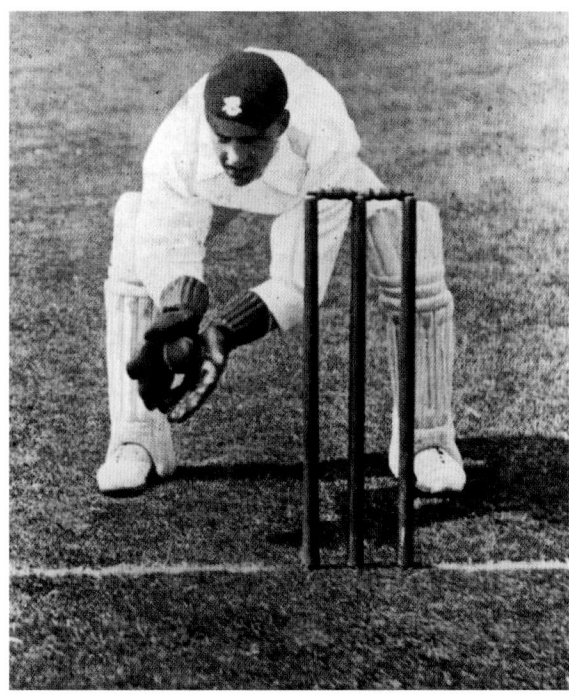

ABOVE An 'action' photograph from 1918 featuring the Surrey and England wicket-keeper Herbert Strudwick

ABOVE The Surrey team celebrate in front of a posse of photographers after winning the 2002 County Championship

Their successors in the Luftwaffe had an even more detrimental effect on cricket photography. Between the wars, photographic rights at Test grounds were sold to two agencies. Sport and General were the organisation that officially had all rights at Lord's and Headingley, but a German bomb destroyed their archive during the 1939-45 war.

Not everything was lost, however, because while the official agencies operated inside the grounds, unofficial photographers perched themselves on buildings outside the perimeter. Using what were in some instances actual pieces of ex-military equipment, they could shoot the action through what were known as 'long tom' lenses.

Still photography has developed rapidly in recent years, with glass plates giving way to digital images and zoom lenses producing photographs of breathtaking clarity. There has been a parallel development when relaying the moving picture. Instead of the jerky images in grainy sepia, we now see television pictures from around the world in perfect colour and from every conceivable angle.

Apart from the spectacular imagery that is broadcast onto television screens,

developed. Both sides rushed through programmes to meet the demand, but it has to be said that the Kaiser's men were very slow to realise the potential for applying their work to cricket!

the effect of the new technology has allowed a much closer insight into the subtleties of cricket. The high-powered zoom lenses take the viewer from his armchair into a very privileged position right in the middle of the action. It means that the intricacies of the game – for so long shrouded by distance – can now be observed, and with increased insight comes enhanced enjoyment.

The advantages of such close encounters available through these zoom lenses, while appreciated by the viewer, have not always met with the universal approval of the players. There are occasions when they might feel that the cameras are intruding into their private space. Naturally such sentiments are particularly prevalent when the players are caught transgressing, but the expression "trial by television" does have some justification.

One of the first such cases occurred in 1992 when Pakistan visited England. Ball-tampering had been known to exist to varying degrees ever since bowlers had tried to make sure the condition of the ball was most favourable to them. When it is within acceptable bounds, little notice is taken of it. However, if it gets out of hand something has to be done.

The two fast bowlers, Wasim Akram and Waqar Younis, were at the peak of their powers, getting the ball to move considerably and at great pace. Fulsome praise was paid to their abilities – until the television cameras zoomed in on the state of the ball. So tight was the close-up, it was evident that when the bowler

LEFT A rare wartime photograph of Gloucestershire and England's Wally Hammond batting at Lord's

was supposedly polishing the ball, his index finger was working away furiously at scratching the surface.

The authorities reacted by bringing in procedures whereby the ball had to be returned to the umpire, both at the fall of a wicket and whenever he asked to see it. That gave the officials the opportunity to monitor how the ball was deteriorating naturally, and to spot any sudden change that might have been attributable to outside influences.

It was a television close-up that brought yet another instance of ball-tampering to public attention. It was a different type of work on the ball that embarrassed Michael Atherton at Lord's in 1994 when England were playing South Africa. The example of Waqar Younis and Wasim Akram had shown that reverse swing was a potent weapon in the modern game, yet on the lush English outfields it was not easy to get the ball into a condition that encouraged it to move in the required fashion.

To achieve reverse swing, one side of the ball should be weighed down with perspiration, while the other should be as dry as possible and preferably rough. To assist with this process, Atherton, the England captain at the time, was

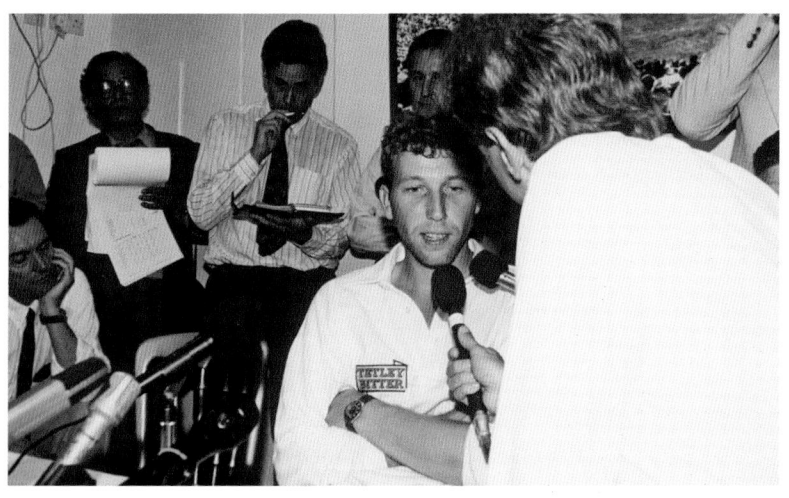

seen applying something to the ball, presumably to assist in this process. As soon as he was detected, the cameras zoomed in to show him taking dirt from his pocket and applying it to the side of the ball.

It was an action that cost Atherton £2,000. The match referee, Peter Burge, took no action against the England captain under Law 42.5 – using an artificial substance to alter the condition of the ball - as Atherton said he had nothing in his pocket. He later admitted that he had been carrying some dirt to keep his hands, and the ball, dry.

Whether dirt was deemed to be an artificial substance in the strictest sense was never tested. Nevertheless, England manager Raymond Illingworth imposed the fine, stating that half was for using the dirt and half for telling a lie to the match referee. The South Africans made no official complaint and the umpires stated that the condition of ball had not been changed, but Atherton's reputation was shot down in flames – just like some of those reconnaissance aircraft over the trenches 80 years earlier.

The pictures in this book were provided courtesy of the following:

GETTY IMAGES
101 Bayham Street, London NW1 0AG

PATRICK EAGAR PHOTOGRAPHY
No 1 Queensberry Place, Friars Lane, Richmond, Surrey TW9 1NW

Photograph of the X-ray of the Ashes urn and Laws of Cricket book courtesy of MCC

Book design and artwork by Darren Roberts

Published by Green Umbrella

Series Editors Jules Gammond, Tim Exell, Vanessa Gardner

Written by Stephen Lamb and Ralph Dellor

With special thanks to Frank Davis at The Lord's Taverners, Clare Skinner and Iain
Wilton at the MCC, Lynda Cole and Patrick Eagar at Patrick Eagar Photography